The Vale of the White Horse is an a
both history & legend. It was here th
the Rings were dreamed, where the
wandered and where one of the most recent Polymaths fed his
giraffe whilst taking tea with Salvador Dali.
But also, it is a thriving place with communities, with
innovative hi-tec companies discovering and making things
that might be better understood by the Ancient Gods at the
Wayland Smithy than by us: mere mortals.
Nick Elwell

Acknowledgements

Editorial Team

Heather Brown
Nick Elwell
Trudy Godfrey
Oliver O'Dell
Daniel Pullen Walenn
Stuart Roper
Dawn Stephens

Contributors

Dr John Sandalls
Jean Sutherland
Heather Armitage
Mike Jones
Emily Sharp
Jonathan Storer
David Collins
Linda Benton
Lynn Barden
Joyce Bunting
Dr Kevin Knowles
Nann Pratt
Liz Rothschild
Howard Hill
Charles Clement
Angela Cousins
Peter Burgess

Lendon Scantlebury
Charles Pappenheim
Andrew Sargent
Peggy Martin
Roger Martin
Sylvia Athawes
Terry Fraser
Ben Carpenter
Alistair Philips
Angela Dearlove
Gill Smith
Cleveland W Gibson
Tracy Wallis
Pauline Cox
Dawn Stephens
Norman Francis
Sally Wallington

Andrew Moore
Peter D Purbrick
Joan L Carter
Anne-Marie Sworn
Brian Hook
Al Cane
Ian Campbell

Mrs J Welsh
Dylan Godfrey
Abigail Brown
Mervyn Powell
Uffington Museum Curator
Adele Vincent
Tracy Wallis

Swan Upping photos by Catherine Hadler, Creative Commercial Photography
Earth Trust photographs by: Ben Carpenter, Alistair Philips, David Hall, Caroline Robson

The editorial team have reserved the right to edit some of the submissions for the overall benefit of the publication.

Introduction

This book grew from a desire to celebrate this beautiful bit of Middle England where we live. The following pages reflect not only where we are —but what we are. The pictures, photographs, prose and poetry all blend to capture the spirit of the time and place important to the contributor.

Much of this book has been generated through the entries into a competition, run locally, inviting those who live or work within The Vale of the White Horse to submit their dreams.

Our aspiration has always been to create a book that one might, every now and again, dip into: to look for inspiration, peace and quiet or something to do or somewhere to explore: far, far away from the madding beaches.

You could spend an entire year discovering this vale and its hidden treasures!

Wayland's Smithy, Ray Gigg

Wayland's Smithy

Slumbering soundly
Within this sylvan coven
Lies lonely Volund,
Blacksmith to the Saxon gods,
His mythic anvil silent.

Mike Jones
Winner of the 52 things Poetry competition

Westmill Thoughts

With engineering elegance
And towering, shimmering brilliance,
These modern windmills stand
In line across bold Adam's land,
A proud and stately band.

The nesting skylarks pay no heed –
They fly and sing, and young chicks feed,
In harmony with man.
And mewing buzzards overhead
The gentle zephyrs fan.

The wheat is waving in the field,
Although no grain these windmills yield –
Free energy they win.
Year long they harvest as they spin,
Wind-power to gather in.

Mike Jones

Westmill Wind Farm is just off the A420 between Swindon and Faringdon.

Coming from Faringdon, take the third exit at the Watchfield Roundabout and continue forward. Take the next right signposted Sevenhampton, Highworth B4508. Westmill is immediately on your right.

Westmill Wind Farm
Kevin Knowles - Winner of the 52 things Photo competition

Faringdon Tour

"Well here we are folks, in Faringdon," the guide Jarge Benson said, his voice full of excitement, "right at the Gateway to the Cotswolds. Our coach will stop here in Sudbury House car park for a couple of hours.

You'll have time to get a cup of coffee, and maybe see a Dragon. So be on your guard!

"Never been here before? Good Lord! Then you've got a treat in store. Just give me a few minutes and I'll tell you all about Faringdon. Any questions?"

"What's that tall tower over there?" elderly Miss Weaver asked. She pointed.

"That there is the Folly Tower. It's about 104 feet high and had a light stuck on top to celebrate the Millennium. Proper bit of engineering job it was. I heard tell planes leaving Heathrow could see the light from 35,000 feet up. It got more famous than the Dome in London."

"Who built the Folly?" Swindon's vicar Peter Brookes asked.

"A chap called Lord Berners. He was well known for his writing, music and paintings. In about 1935 he got the tower built with a Gothic piece stuck on the top. He was an eccentric with a wicked dry sense of humour. I heard he often invited celebrities for fancy dress parties. Famous? Sure. He got mentioned in Time Magazine and London Review. Take a good look around and you'll see special pigeons painted in his Berners colours like pink, yellow and purple.

"History says the Romans built a wooden fort on Folly Hill. Records show thousands of legionnaires marched past Faringdon on their way to Oxford, Chester and Hadrian's Wall. Must have been some sight. Just imagine it, seeing the Romans march past in full uniforms and with all their weapons. Fantastic colours; enough to get the blood going.

"Sometimes the soldiers would spot a dragon and light a beacon to warn fellow Romans camped on Uffington Hill. You see this really is dragon country and the scared folks had to supply blonde virgins as human sacrifice. However, good ole St George killed the dragon on Dragon Hill. Some battle!"

"Were there any other wars fought here?" ex-RAF pilot Steve Maddon asked."

"Sure, remember Oliver Cromwell? He dragged his gun battery to the top of Folly Hill to challenge the town. Then he let his gunners demolish the spire to All Saints Church. After that, he ordered Faringdon House to be seized. The attack was defeated forcing Cromwell to retreat. Years later the Sealed Knot came to town to re-enact a battle. Now it's fun to watch the soldiers in the Market Place firing their cannons and muskets."

"Faringdon House was also made famous by Pye, the poet, who wrote the nursery rhyme about four and twenty blackbirds baked in a pie. It drove mad King George up the wall."

"If you stroll down London Street take a look at the Folly pub. I heard you can always get a free drink there. Mind you, the free drink is water but there you are. Do you like spicy hot cross buns? Then buy some from Lillian in the bakery halfway down London Street. Well worth a visit."

"For pleasant surroundings try sitting on the bench by the Portwell. Take in the atmosphere of the Market Place. The Old Town Hall has been converted and often has an excellent display of paintings. If you fancy some beer try the Bell Hotel or the Old Crown Coaching Inn. There is also the new Portwell Angel bar where some nights you can enjoy opera or cheeky French and Italian acts while you sit around a table eating pasta and drinking red wine."

"Now you may not believe it but there is a series of tunnels that run underground from All Saints Church to Folly Hill and to the Old Crown Coaching Inn. It's too difficult to check out these days. Ghosts? Sure you always get ghosts in a historic place like Faringdon. There is supposed to be one in the graveyard by All Saints Church. Some drunks claim to have seen ghostly figures but that is another story.
As you're in the Market Place why not pop into the shops. Buy a postcard. Grab some brochures. Read about this here historic Faringdon and the hanging judge Jefferies. All intriguing stuff.

"Let's all meet back at the coach in two hours time. Ok." ***

"Well folks, welcome back on board the coach. Did you have a great time?"

"Good, I'm glad that you all enjoyed your visit so far to Faringdon. But we haven't finished yet.

"Now it so happens I've got a feeling something strange might happen on this trip to dragon country. I feels it in me bones.

"Here, let me tell you what I've got in store for you this afternoon. Hold onto your hats because I'm going to take you to all sorts of places of interest.

"Now we're on the move, you'll notice the signs for Buscot. That's where we're heading to take a look at this National Trust house and park. Inside Buscot House are many fine paintings. Look in your brochures and you'll see what I mean. There are illustrations so fine you'll stop and stare. Remember the tale of Sleeping Beauty. Well, see the famous painting for yourself.

"As we're stopping at Buscot why not take a walk up to the weir. It's quite an exciting place. Look at all the boats navigating the Thames and watch them go through the lock. If you get hungry with all this country air you can nip along to the tea room for a piece of chocolate cake.

"After Buscot I thought we could go to Coleshill and then back towards Faringdon. Up a steep hill and stop at Badbury Clumps. It's a smashing place for walking and relaxing. I've often gone there to picnic. People walk their dog or go there to jog. Everyone loves the bluebells in the woods.

"Seeing as Great Coxwell is so close I thought we'd press on to the Great Tithe Barn. We could stop at the building and take a look. The barn was built about 1205 and run by Cistercian monks. Proper lively place it was, especially at harvest time when the monks brought out jugs of ale for the workers. Tithing was the in thing and the monks helped the poor of the parish in hard times. The tithe money came from the annual harvest. When we get there you can see the size of the barn. Imagine it was full of wheat, barley, corn and stuff to feed the animals in the winter. Take a look at the massive beams. Impressive.

"Now when we've finished with the barn I thought we could next head out towards the White Horse at Uffington. We can stop in the car park, not far from the white horse cut in chalk. Take your camera. From where the White Horse is situated the ground just plunges away. Look at the road some hundreds of feet below. Just the other side of the road is the mound where St George killed the Dragon. It's a place to remember. Without the battle we'd have no St George and where would England be without its patron saint? If you fancy buying souvenirs you can get them from the caravan park run by Ashdown House. Some of you might want to look at Wayland's Smithy. If so, come along with me and I'll take you there.

"After we have finished at Uffington we'll head back to Faringdon. If there is time we will call in at the Faringdon Leisure Centre. I really want to show off the swimming pool. Now the manager has agreed to take us on a tour of the centre so we'll be able to see all of the facilities. I'm sure you will be impressed.

"By the time we have finished at the Leisure Centre we are all going to be hungry. I suggest that we use the Portwell Angel in the Market Place to get some energy back.

"Now are there any questions?"

"Jarge! Jarge! Look! Up there in the sky. The black dot with flames and smoke pouring from it. What do you make of that?" the Swindon vicar shouted.

"Remember I said something strange might happen. I just happened to feel it in me bones."

"Sure. But it's heading this way and getting bigger." Miss Weaver returned.

**"You're right.
Then folks just panic; meet your first dragon!"**

Cleveland Gibson - Winner of the 52 things Prose competition

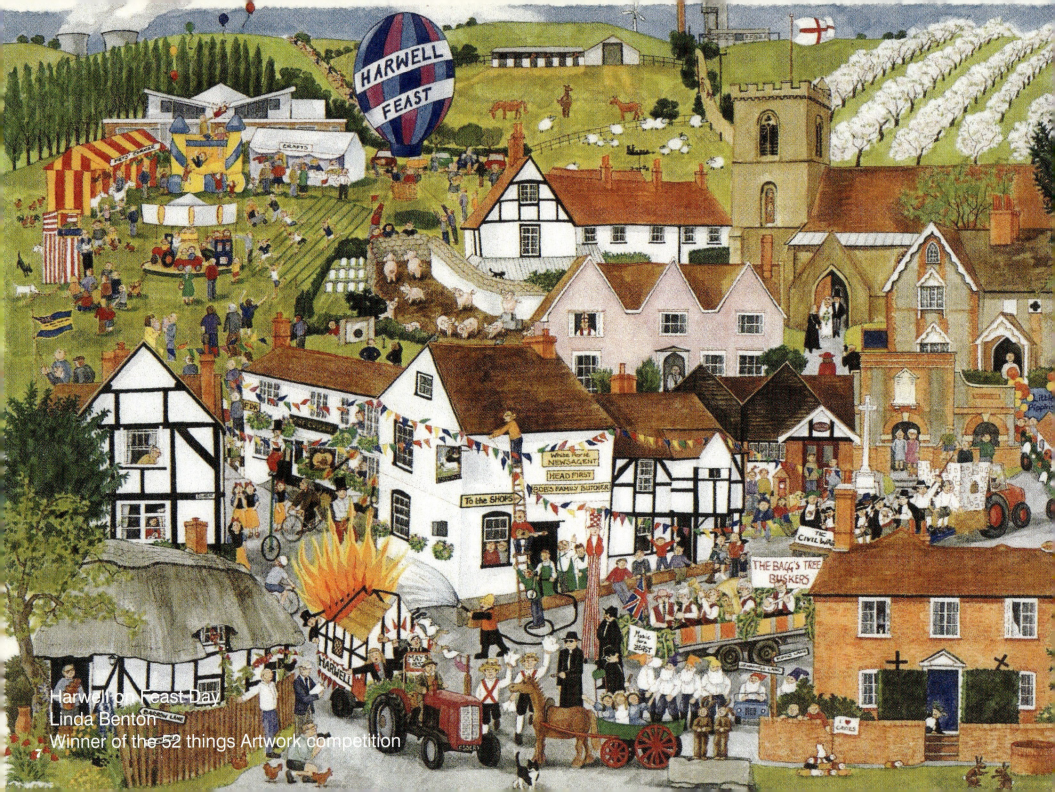

Harwell on Feast Day
Linda Benton
Winner of the 52 things Artwork competition

Our Village Fete

Once a year in August, we had a lovely treat,
For on our village green there came a little Fair complete.
A wonderful array of stalls, hooplas, shies and swings,
As seen through the eyes of children, there's magic in such things.

The vans came rumbling down our street quite early in the day,
We all rushed round to the village green, the feast had come to stay.
There was Old Liza, small and brown, a walnut sort of face,
All wrinkled up and weather tanned with a shawl on, made of lace.

There was big Harry, strong and tall, he swung the hammer to
put up the stall,
Then dear old Sukie, rushing about getting all her coconuts out.
She placed them each in their little arm chairs and, throw as you might,
they still sat there,
They were brown and round and oh so sweet, if ever you managed
to get one to eat.

"Throw the balls at 'em – give 'em a blow" then pay another sixpence and
have another go,
Up went the Hoop-la, what a wonderful display, "clocks of all descriptions for
you to win and play".
Well, now off again I go to have a swing up high, down low,
The awful motion makes me giddy, but I still go up with my friend Billy.

Up and up we go so high, it seems to me I could touch the sky,
Then down we clamber, back to ground, and have a ride on the
Merry-go-Round.
A little pony makes it go, it trots for fast and walks for slow,
The organ plays a merry tune, oh why must I go home so soon?

Oh mustn't forget the Jumbo Feast, brandy snaps and liquorice sweets,
Jumbo's fat, sticky and sweet, covered in wasps, but such a treat.
Round once more before I go, someone's calling "Come on Flo!"

I rush over and find that Billy has won a prize, a china filly.
Now the flares are all in place, doesn't the light seem to alter face,
The shadows dance around the stall, it isn't the Village Green at all.
It's some strange place I do not know, I'm a little tired so home I go,
Tomorrow I'll come to an empty green, almost as if it has never been.

But there in the grass I see it was true, the tracks of the pony, dear little Sue,
Her hoofs have worn the grass away, in a magic circle, its there to stay.
It's proof to me that on August Ten,
The wonderful feast will be back again.

The age we live in now is changed, the Feast is long since dead,
But in my heart I treasure it, and also in my head.
I think of all the wonderous things that can be done today,
But the joys of a Feast on my village green will never fade away.

I wonder do they miss us, Old Liza, Sukie, Joe,
I guess they are in green pastures now, twas all so long ago.
But oh my friends believe me, the happiness I had,
With a tiny pile of coppers and a little friendly lad.

A ride together in a swing, a Jumbo each to chew,
I wonder do you think of me, as I remember you.
The village green still stands there, no hoof prints mar the grass,
But the village is a poorer place now that the feast has passed.

Sarah Lay

Morris Men - Linda Benton

Abingdon

Abingdon, sometimes called Abingdon on Thames, has a strong claim to be England's oldest town. Archaeological digs show this was one of the earliest areas where our hunter-gatherer ancestors first began to lead more settled lifestyles, attracted by the food and trading opportunities of the confluence of the River Ock with the River Thames. Medieval Abingdon was a significant place. From the time of Abbot Aethelwold, c. 943-963, the Abbey of St Mary's was a centre of excellence in the cultural and religious life of Europe. Its lands, wealth and learning were managed by Benedictine monks, but relations with the little town, which had begun to grow in front of the abbey, were not always good. The archway which once formed the entrance to the abbey grounds can still be seen today. There were times when the gates had to be locked against the rioting townsfolk.

St Nicolas' church belonged to the abbey but faced out to the town. Known as the "little church by the gate", it was built so that the servants and ordinary people who were connected with the abbey could receive Holy Communion whilst being firmly kept out of the abbey itself.

The St Helen's area developed as one of the principal trading wharves on this part of the Thames and the medieval houses of East St Helen's Street were the homes of the town's successful merchant and business families. In St Helen's Church they set up a decorative cross which was the focal point for their independence from the abbey. The Fraternity of the Holy Cross was a committee devoted to the management of problems like the care of the poor and the maintenance of infrastructure for the common good. They built almshouses such as Long Alley and constructed the main bridge over the Thames.

St Helen's Church is unusual. It is almost square inside rather than the usual oblong shape, due to repeated additions of one oblong nave followed by another as the enthusiastic townsfolk of Abingdon added to their church and raised its status a little at a time. It is now a treasure of great importance to the town containing medieval ceiling paintings, a panorama of stained glass windows and one of the earliest known family tree paintings.

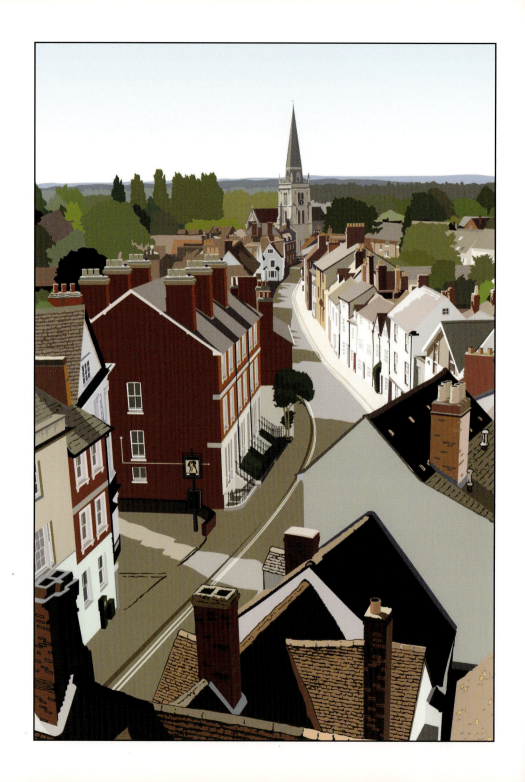

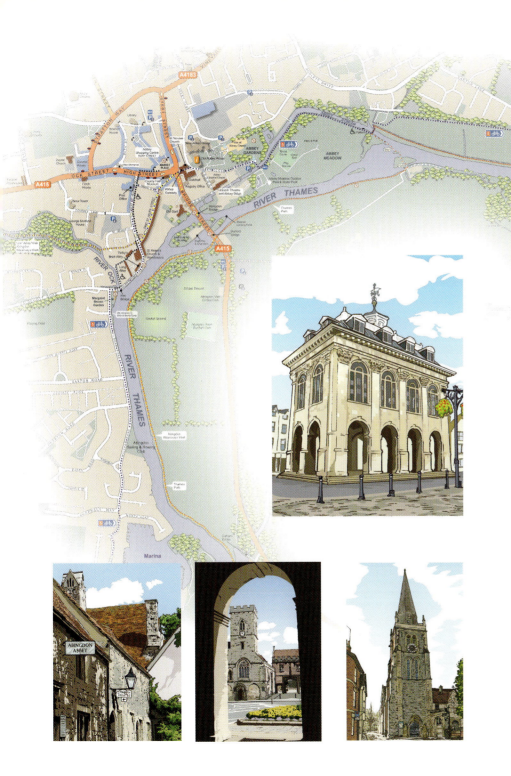

The growing importance of the town was reflected in the design of the County Hall, erected between 1678 and 1684. Christopher Kempster's building seems to draw heavily on the work of Sir Christopher Wren and today it is a museum housing local exhibits and a craft collection.

The Old Gaol, completed in 1811, was built possibly using a workforce of Napoleonic prisoners of war. The strange octagonal design with three wings was part of a new enlightened approach to prison management. The cells were placed in the easily-managed wing-blocks allowing all to have windows for light and fresh air.

The Abbey Buildings still survive, saved by the Friends of Abingdon in 1944. Local volunteers created the Elizabethan-style Unicorn Theatre which opened in time for Elizabeth II's coronation in 1953. Today, professional and amateur productions take on a unique quality from their intimate setting.

Heather Brown

Illustrations - Peter Bellingham

Peter Bellingham is an illustrator, cartoonist and designer. Having studied in Shropshire and North Wales, he has worked on illustration projects for companies such as Volvo, British Gas, Virgin and the NHS.

Wantage

"Wantage has the most beautiful Market Place. It took my breath away the first time I saw it. Surrounded by ancient buildings, in particular on the South and West, you could be forgiven for thinking you were in a world long gone. On a Sunday, when it is quieter, you can almost hear the sound of the animal markets, the hustle and bustle of the people in their work and the horses and carts passing through."

Wantage was an ancient Roman settlement and birthplace of King Alfred the Great. A statue in his memory was erected in 1876, two years after the demolition of the Old Town Hall, and presented to the Town by Colonel Loyd Linsay (later Lord Wantage). The new town hall was opened in 1878 and is now the HSBC bank. The Bell Inn across the road from this building is one of the oldest pubs in the town and was partly owned by churchwardens.

According to Stiles Genealogy:
"There has been a church in Wantage since the mid 10th century. The present church of St Peter and St Paul dates from three hundred years later and is the oldest building in the town, although there have been many changes and additions to it since.

The manor of Wantage once belonged to the Fitzwaryns. The church contains the 1360s tomb of Sir William and Amicia Fitzwaryn, and there is a full-size brass of Sir Ivo Fitzwarin, their son, dated 1414. Sir Ivo has been immortalised as 'Baron Fitzwarren' the father of Lady Alice who married Dick Whittington. The main residence of the Fitzwaryns was actually at Castle Whittington in Shropshire."

There are many examples of fine Queen Anne and Georgian architecture in Wantage, some covering older buildings. The Bear Hotel on the south side of the Market Place is an Old Coaching Inn and part of it dates from the early 17th century. The Blue Boar round the corner was a stopping point for the sheep drovers that came through this town. There are numerous fascinating bits of information and things of interest to look for on many frontages. Take some time and see what you can find, such as a plaque on the wall relating to the Post Office Vaults. There used to be a town pond at the East end of the market square. It is now covered over, but vaulted and there is access from a cover in front of the Post Office Vaults.

The thriving Market Place was for buying and selling livestock, corn, flour, malt and coal. The Wessex Flour Mill down Mill Street still produces locally sourced flour of excellent quality and is adjacent to where the Wharf used to be. The Sack Hiring Company office that was here used to organise the transportation of flour from Wantage Mill along the Berkshire and Wiltshire canal. The sack house remains and has recently been refurbished.

There were many tanneries in this town, Grove Street and Priory Road were known for them and the name "Black Wantage" may have come from these: or perhaps from the fact that criminals from London used to escape down here using the canals!

There is a wealth of information about this wonderful Market Town available but nothing can beat walking around and experiencing the history first hand.

Dawn Stephens

From Oxford:
Head west out of Oxford along the A420. At Tubney Wood Roundabout take the first exit onto the A338. At WilliamsF1 roundabout take the first exit onto the A338 signposted Wantage and A417. At roundabout take first exit onto A338. Turn right. Turn right onto A417.

From Swindon:

Take A420 towards Faringdon. At Stanford roundabout take the second exit onto A417 signposted Wantage. At roundabout take second exit onto A417. At mini-roundabout bear left immediately. At mini-roundabout bear right onto A417 signposted town centre.

Ashbury Down

By summer, the downs outside the village of Ashbury are unspoiled wild meadows. My favourite time to visit is winter when the landscape is transformed by snow to a winter wonderland.

White Horse Hill

This Iron Age fortress guards an ancient highway,
Its ramparts now the home of humble sheep,
Three thousand years the scene of human conflict,
Its only sentry now a bird of prey.

The sparrow-hawk on lonely hawthorn sitting
In sheltered hollow 'midst the timeless hills
Surveys with keenest eye, on small birds preying –
Beware blithe skylark, yellowhammer, finch.

The White Horse, mystic logo of this land,
Forever prances up the hillside steep,
Performs its magic each midsummer's night
For all who dare to rest within its eye.

Below, a hill bears witness to a myth
Of dragon slayed by great and fearless George,
No grass will grow on these stark patches, white,
Where spilled his blood, or so the legend tells.

And in the East a modern temple lies,
Monument to twentieth century man,
Its cooling towers, seen for miles around,
Spew clouds of steam into the wintry sky.

Yet all of this is more than panorama,
More, much more than just a pretty view -
A sense of history this place conveys
To those who would discern its charms profound.

Mike Jones

White Horse Hill

The White Horse of Uffington is thought to be the oldest hill figure in Britain. The stylised image, nearly four hundred feet in length, may date from 1000BC in the late Bronze Age. It is thought that the figure could represent a horse goddess connected with the local Belgae tribe. This goddess is generally believed to be one form of Epona, worshipped throughout the Celtic world.

During the Iron Age, animals and particularly horses held important symbolic meaning beyond their immediate worth as valued possessions. Evidence from ritual burials on Blewburton Hill reinforces this belief and conjures up an intense mental picture of our area at this time.

Taken from "A View from the Hill" edited by Peter Cockrell and Shirley Kay

Slightly irrelevantly, perhaps, it has recently been mooted that the White Horse was actually (originally?) a dragon. Perhaps a horse with wings might be mistaken for a dragon. Who knows!

The X47 bus run by RH transport goes from Wantage to Swindon stopping at White horse hill. You can also get to Wantage via the X30 bus run by Stagecoach.

From Wantage, follow the B4507 then turn left when prompted by a brown sign for White Horse Hill and Waylands Smithy. (OX12 9 for sat nav)

Authors in the Vale

The Vale area boasts many literary associations. Thomas Hardy set one of his most famous novels 'Jude the Obscure' in Letcombe Bassett where 'Arabella's Cottage' can still be seen. In the novel Wantage is thinly disguised as Alfredston and Oxford as Christminster. Dean Jonathan Swift lived at The Old Rectory in Letcombe which dates back to the C17th, with a large thatched barn which dates back to around 1400. In the garden of the Rectory is the mulberry tree under which Dean Swift sat while writing some of his famous satires.

Author of '1984' and 'Animal Farm', George Orwell is buried in the churchyard at Sutton Courtenay in a grave given by the Astor family. Sir Compton Mackenzie, author of 'Whisky Galore' lived at East Hanney near Wantage.

The Poet Laureate, Sir John Betjeman, lived in Uffington and Wantage where he set his children's book, Archie and the Strict Baptists. The first Wantage Betjeman Festival of Literature and Poetry was held in September 2011. This week long event featured talks from over 30 writers and poets as well as Betjeman and Hardy walks, films and musical entertainments. It is hoped to make this an annual event celebrating the rich cultural history of the town and surrounding villages.

The Betjeman Millennium Park in Wantage contains a series of sculptures carved with lines from his poems. Also worth a visit a few miles down the road, is the beautiful memorial window, designed by John Piper, set in All Saints' Church in Farnborough, Berkshire, where Betjeman lived in the adjoining Rectory.

The White Horse has inspired many artists such as Eric Ravilious, Henry Moore and Paul Nash as well as writers, from Chesterton's poetry to Thomas Hughes (of Tom Brown's Schooldays fame) who was born in Uffington. Contemporary writers living in and writing about the Vale include Eliza Graham and Candida Lycett Green, John Betjeman's daughter. Writer and poet Pam Ayres was born in nearby Stanford in the Vale.
Author Guy Browning's recent film Tortoise in Love is a romantic comedy filmed at Kingston Bagpuize House, which is open to visitors, near Abingdon.

Old Berks Point to Point, Lockinge

Held annually on Easter Monday, Point to Point Steeplechasing is an amateur sport. It provides a crucial link for many amateur riders and trainers, with ambition, to turn professional. Point to Point at Lockinge has been going for more than fifty years with The Queen having had runners competing and former champion jockey Richard Dunwoody having had his first English race here. The event provides plenty of family friendly activities. It includes an open-to-all dog show and a diverse array of trade stands that include beer tents, food stalls and popular retail brands. As well as plenty of opportunities to shop there is, of course, the Bookmakers and a Tote. It is an ideal occasion to enjoy a family day out in our beautiful country-side and to appreciate the thrills and spills of a course covering nearly three miles, over eighteen fences.

Goodlake Barns

"A base for exploring the heart of England, a peaceful retreat in the Oxfordshire countryside"

Goodlake Barns are award winning self-catering cottages situated on an organic farm arranged together around a courtyard in the picturesque village of Shellingford. This is a relaxing place to stay and a convenient base for exploring the Vale of the White Horse and the wider area.

The series of light and spacious self catering cottages are sensitively converted, retaining much of the character and charm of the original stone barns, stables and outbuildings.

The stables at Church Farm were constructed in the mid 19th century when the manor of Shellingford was part of a large agricultural estate and the lord of the manor was a Thomas Mills Goodlake. It is his initials that are inscribed on the stables and from whom the name originates.

There are five cottages of varying sizes, arranged close together around a courtyard in the centre of the village close to the church. This is a place where friends and family can stay together and unwind in a beautifully location and plenty of opportunities to explore the area and take up activities such as fishing, golf and riding.

www.goodlakebarns.co.uk
Tel: 01367 710112

Gerald Hugh Tyrwhitt-Wilson, 14th Baron Berners 1883 – 1950

Called the 'last great eccentric' he was a composer, painter, and novelist, who dyed his flock of doves different colours. He often put up silly signs such as 'Please do not feed the giraffes'. He also wrote his own epitaph

> Here lies Lord Berners
> One of the learners
> His great love of learning
> May earn him a burning
> But praise to the lord
> He seldom was bored

Lord Berners' ashes are buried in the lawn at Faringdon House.

He said:
'There is a good deal to be said for frivolity. Frivolous people, when all is said and done, do less harm in the world than some of our philanthropisers and reformers.
Mistrust a man who never has an occasional flash of silliness.'

During the 1930s and 1940s Faringdon House was known to host some of the best weekend parties in the South of England. Lord Berners visitors included: Stravinsky, Salvador Dali, George Bernard Shaw, John Betjeman, Nancy Astor and the Mitford sisters.

Lord Berners, built the Folly Tower for his friend Robert Heber-Percy. It was opened on 5th November 1935. In 1982 Robert Heber-Percy gave the tower and woodland to the people of Faringdon. Faringdon Folly Trust have opened it to the public since 1985.

Faringdon Folly Tower

Folly Hill is one of a number of Lower Greensand hills. It was formed over 100 million years ago, in the Cretaceous period. Before the Roman Conquest of 43 AD there was a hill fort on Faringdon Hill. It had commanding views over the Vale of the White Horse and Thames Valley.

'Faringdon' derived from Ferendune, the fern covered hill, as recorded in the Domesday survey of 1086. In the battle of Faringdon in 1145, King Stephen defeated Matilda, the mother of Henry II. He destroyed the wooden fort on Faringdon hill.

In the Civil War (1642-1651) Oliver Cromwell failed in his attack on the Royalists at Faringdon House. Some believe Cromwell destroyed the church steeple, others believe it was demolished by the Royalists to hinder an assault on Faringdon House.

Henry James Pye (1745-1813) lived in Faringdon House. He was dubbed the worst poet laureate ever, such that he was lampooned by his peers in the nursery rhyme 'Sing a Song of Sixpence'. He planted the Scots Pine on Folly Hill and some said this was the most creative thing he did. Some of these trees are still standing.

During World War II the Folly Tower and Hill were used as a Home Guard lookout and for wireless exercises. The Hill has had various names through the ages including: Faringdon Hill, Cromwell's Battery, Unton's Folly, Pye's Folly, Lord Berners' Folly and Folly Hill.

My favourite Hallowe'en night was the time we went up Faringdon Folly Tower. There was spooky music playing and ghosts and witches everywhere! We climbed 104 steps up the Folly Tower in the dead of night with torches to light our way, to the sound of ghastly and ghostly noises coming from every direction. And on the way out, we got some sweets! A lovely Hallowe'en night.
Dylan Godfrey (age 7).
www.faringdonfolly.org.uk

From Oxford

Take A420 towards Faringdon. About 2 miles after Littleworth, take a right signed Faringdon Market Square, Folly Hill. Soon after Sudbury House take a turning left. You will see a high pavement on the left. The footpath to the Folly is off this by the railings. You can park further up this road (it is a dead end) or in a car park in the town.

From Swindon

Take A420 towards Faringdon. About 1.5 miles from Faringdon pass the Great Coxwell and Faringdon Town Centre turns. Continue along by pass taking a left turn signed to Faringdon Market Square, Folly Hill. Soon after Sudbury House take a turning left. You will see a high pavement on the left. The footpath to the Folly is off this by the railings. You can park further up this road (it is a dead end) or in a car park in the town.

It's all Art About Abingdon

I love to be surprised by interesting objects and artworks that add intrigue and individuality to a place.

Abingdon has been fortunate in recent years to have a number of new artworks commissioned. There is a lovely collection of contemporary public art, that isn't too obscure or abstract. Most works are about Abingdon or the surrounding area reflecting its history, local people and uniqueness.

A map and explanations of this wonderful collection called 'Art About Abingdon' can be found in the main reception of the District Council building and the Tourist information point at the Town Council offices.

Abigail Brown

The Wantage Tramway

In eighteen-hundred and seventy-three
There issued from Wantage a new decree
Railways are running all over the land
It's high time we joined that merry band!
A Meeting was held in Wantage Town Hall
Chaired by Loyd Linsay, assisted by all
Those people in Berkshire who lived close by
And came to the meeting, though some asked, Why?
They conferred together and all agreed
A line to Wantage is what we need,
To carry freight from the station at Grove
An excellent plan so it is, by Jove!
And passengers too, there is a great need
(Though it will not travel at much of a speed.)

With thinking caps on the plans were made
And so work began, land levelled, rails laid.
The line ran by the Besselsleigh Turnpike
So no longer would anyone need to hike!
The Surveyor was from Abingdon
(Do you think he ever threw a bun?)
Edward Dolby was his name
The Engineer was of local fame
George Stevenson from Wantage Baptist Church
He would not leave them in the lurch!
We must have a name, so what do you say
Then one piped up, The Wantage Tramway!

We really should have an engine to pull
And that must be made as strong as a bull
From the South to the North they searched the land
And eventually one came to hand
Shunting trains in a siding in Crewe.
After inspecting and having a view

A Loco was bought then, Shannon her name
And over her life she achieved great fame
She pulled all the wagons with might and main
Though folks from Wantage rechristened her Jane!
She's now one of Didcot's railway displays
Having travelled the country that's where she stays.

And people from Wantage were filled with pride
The first tramway to use Steam for the ride!
Though folks by the track with roofs made of thatch
Stood by with buckets of water to latch
On to those sparks that could start a fire
A situation that would be so dire!

Then through the years the motor-car came
And passenger numbers were never the same
And so, in nineteen-hundred and twenty-five
There were no more passengers, dead or alive!

In nineteen forty-five it came to pass
That the line had to close, alack, alas
It had reached the years of mortal span
Well it would if it had been a man!

And that was the end of the Wantage Tramway
It had served its purpose for many a day
Carried people and freight from Wantage to Grove
Perhaps some on their way to Brighton and Hove!

Jean Sunderland
abridged version

The Abingdon Walk Series

When most towns put out a walk guide it tends to be a few instructions and a sketch map. For anyone wanting to explore the countryside around Abingdon, there is a series of guides being published that promise to be a lot more.

Abingdon is unusual for a town of its size in being closely connected to the rural landscape on two sides. Today's visitors can thank the geography of the river flood plains for the lack of urban sprawl; from admiring the medieval heart of the town round St Helens Church, a walker can be out in the open countryside within minutes, with a fine round trip of several miles of rural landscape dotted with peaceful villages, if you feel inclined. The Waterways Walk is the longest, covering a seven or eight mile route, which takes in Sutton Courtenay and Drayton, including the burial place of George Orwell, but the Two Locks Walk provides a shorter stroll to work up an appetite for lunch or dinner.

This series of walk guides do justice to the rich history embedded in the landscape and are the kind of guides you try to keep dry when you are out because you know you are going to treasure them for fireside reading in the future.

With writing that imbibes a sense of the story behind every lock, bridge or building, and delightful illustrations from artist, Stuart Roper, these guides will be much-loved by visitors and locals alike.

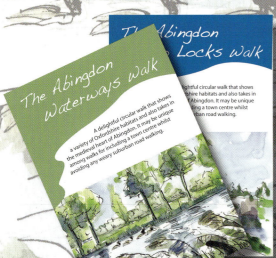

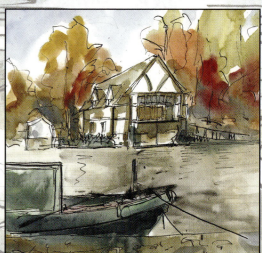

Postcards from the Water's Edge

The Thames is key to understanding our rural landscape and our historical towns. Crossing points developed into thriving towns and river banks became tribal, then county, boundaries. Trade connections developed between wharves like Abingdon and the busy London metropolis, which lasted up until the railway age.

Today, the Thames is a tranquil but interesting linear journey. It offers an ever-unfolding view of wildlife, gardens, pasture, bustling market towns and peaceful villages. From medieval bridges to Georgian locks and weirs, the river holds centuries of engineering ingenuity. Whether you join the friendly boating fraternity or you walk the Thames Path National Trail, the river will tell its story as you travel. Stop off in one of the many pub gardens, fine restaurants and Victorian tea rooms.

Broad Face

A step away from Abingdon Bridge, and close by the last remaining buildings of the medieval abbey, the Broad Face gastro-pub has restored its original inn sign after rediscovering it through a local resident. The name of the pub is thought to be very old, referring to the look of the hanged criminals who met their ends at the Old Gaol opposite, but the inn sign seems to take a more jovial interpretation.

With black rock grill weekday lunches, Sunday roasts with live jazz, and local beers and wines included in their extensive selection, the Broad Face is a must-stop on your Thames journey; break your river bank walk at Abingdon Bridge or tie up at Abingdon's free moorings to enjoy the Broad Face's hospitality (and don't leave without trying the Crème brûlée!)

From Culham take the number 116. From Abingdon take the number 114. From Didcot take the number 32.

From Abingdon take the A34 then the A4183 turn left to Culham bridge and then take a right turn when you get to the Wagon and Horses pub. There should then be a free car park. (OX14 4NE for sat nav)

Artists in the Vale

The Vale of White Horse is a great place for art and artists, and many well-known creative people live and work in this area. Artweeks (www.artweeks.org) is held every year during May when you can visit artists' studios, discuss their work and even purchase from them. A few of these artists also invite you to call them and visit whenever you want to.

Dawn Benson, is a well-known sculptor who exhibits around the UK and has pieces in collections around the world. Dawn produces Bronze and Bronze Resin stylised relationship sculptures and in particular is known for her horse and child sculptures, which she sells throughout the UK in prestigious galleries as well as direct from her studios. Dawn also produces paintings in a variety of media including oils, acrylics, watercolour and mixed media.

Dawn's partner, Lendon Scantlebury is also very well known as a sculptor and painter. Lendon started life in Barbados and he said:

"It has left me with strong memories of the freshness, brightness and vibrant colour of those early years. The people there have a togetherness as a community, because of the small size of the island.

"The memories of the salty sea smells, the heat and the cooking smells all mingled together, have powerful connotations for me. The energy, the colourful facial expressions and the voices provide unforgettable memories.

Coming to England I noticed that everything here is much more muted. In my paintings I try to bring out the bright freshness that I once experienced. The light is so strong and the colours so vibrant, it reminds me of where I came from and who I am. It gives me a sense of well being. We need to take time to notice the changing environment, 'watching the clouds go by' because here we move so fast. I don't hear people talk to each other about those things. In paradise people move slowly, there is no need to hurry. "

www.barwellgallery.co.uk

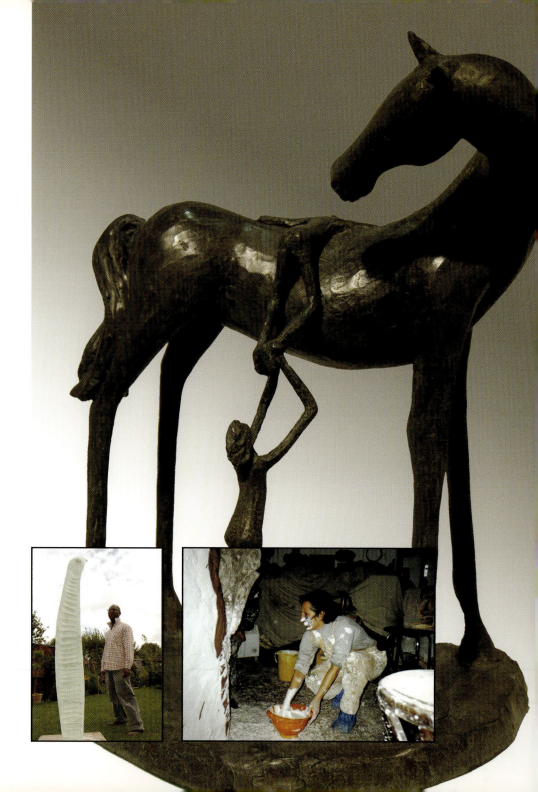

My favourite walk

My favourite walk starts at the Chain Hill car park and leads east towards Hendred. Whether you want a circular walk or a gentle stroll the views are magnificent. I like to walk past the memorial to Lord Wantage while deer spotting or watching the Red Kites aerial display. Then down and through Ardington and finish by walking uphill through the point to point field, back to the start.

Lendon Scantlebury

I love to walk up to Segsbury Camp on the Ridgeway. At the top of the Camp are the most spectacular views for miles around. I like to sit there relaxing and enjoying the ancient landscape and its serene tranquility. From here I can meander around Gramps Hill and through the woods, or sometimes towards the Letcombes. In the spring, the ground is covered in cowslips and I enjoy watching the buzzards hovering high above. Then, gently back to earth, visit the nearby Court Hill tea-rooms, a lovely place for a coffee and cake at the end of a fantastic walk.

Dawn Benson

Fallowfields Hotel and Restaurant

A sweeping drive runs between sunlit lawns and specimen trees, taking us away from the main road and into the tranquility of the rich 12 acres of the Fallowfields Hotel. The cluster of buildings in its centre are full of Victorian charm, while stepping into the main entrance the mix of sophistication and comfort that runs throughout the building's interior becomes immediately apparent.

As our visit continued we would discover that this combination of quality and welcoming defines not only the décor but the business itself. A tour of the estate reveals that every facet has been developed by the independent, family-owned hotel with a personal pride and ethos that is always easy to admire but so often difficult to find.

Leaving the outside eating marquee bathed in summer sun we find ourselves walking over croquet lawns, with swallows swooping overhead. Open for guests to wander in, the grounds are lush and natural, not manicured, while the kitchen garden, fruit orchard and livestock pens are worth a visit in themselves to those interested in ethical and sustainable farming. Beyond the kitchen garden we come across a falconry lesson in progress, a small group hushed by their close encounter with Fallowfield's birds of prey.

Fallowfields hotel at once tranquil, sophisticated and charismatic serves both as an ideal base for those wishing to explore wider Oxfordshire and as a truly memorable destination for families and parties in its own right.

From medlars and quince, to mint and sorrel, to rare breed meats and Dexter beef, newly appointed head chef Shaun Dickens is provided with an enviable selection of ingredients as fresh as any chef or diner could hope for. Boasting Michelin starred experience, Shaun's CV is just as impressive as any of his excellent seasonal menus and his recent appointment has brought a memorable dining experience to the restaurant that, quite justly, is a matter of particular pride to the owners.

Bookings and further information 01865 820416 www.fallowfields.com
Faringdon Road, Kingston Bagpuize with Southmoor,
Oxfordshire OX13 5BH

Kelmscott Manor

One of my favourite places in the west of our area is Kelmscott Manor. It was the home of William Morris – poet, craftsman and socialist – from 1871 until his death in 1896.

Morris is famous as a craftsman, textile designer and his association with the Pre-Raphaelite brotherhood, in particular Edward Burne-Jones and the 'enfant terrible' of the group Dante Gabriel Rossetti. It was Rossetti that introduced Morris to Jane Burden with whom Morris fell head over heels in love and later married. Jane was a great beauty, a self educated artist, the model for many of Rossetti's paintings and later his lover.

The house itself contains many exquisite tapestries and artworks by Morris, Jane and Rossetti and is a joy to behold, set as it is in a beautiful country garden. However, for me it is the room that Rossetti used as a studio that sends a shiver down my spine. When I last visited the house there was a box of the artist's paints lying open on a table, as if he had just left the room. I think it is the complex and painful relationship between the three artists which gives this delightful rural idyll a strange and haunting atmosphere.

Stuart Roper

From the M4 leave at junction 15 and take the A346/A419 exit to A420. At Plough Hill roundabout, take the first exit onto the A419 heading towards Swidon/Oxford/A420. At White Hart roundabout take the third exit onto the A420. Keep left when you get to the fork. At Park Road roundabout take the first exit onto Park Road/A417. Continue to follow A417 and turn right onto Gloucester Street. Turn left onto Church Street. Turn left onto Radcot Road. Continue to follow A4095. Turn left onto Langley Road. Turn left. Then take the first left, then turn right and Kelmscott manor will be on your right. (GL7 3HJ for satnav)

28

The Sculptor of King Alfred

In late 2006, when the right arm of King Alfred's statue was unlawfully removed, Wantage folk were universal in expressing a great sense of sadness and hurt. The statue, which so many of us had admired was looked upon even more affectionately than ever before. But how many of us know about the man who sculpted this magnificent monument?

When the Prince and Princess of Wales (later King Edward VII and Queen Alexandra) unveiled the statue on July 14 1887, standing alongside the prince was the 44 year-old sculptor Count Gleichen.

Count Gleichen was no ordinary man. He was born Prince Victor Ferdinand Franz Eugen Gustaf Constantin Friedrich of Hohenlohe-Langenburg at a castle in the mountains of Wurttemberg in Germany in 1833. In his childhood, Victor enjoyed all the trappings of the aristocracy but this man was no namby pamby. When eventually he was sent to school in Dresden he ran away with the intention of joining the navy, but was caught, returned to school and punished.

When Queen Victoria got to hear about her young relative she suggested he should come to England and join the Royal Navy. He did as she suggested and after naturalisation he joined HMS Powerful as a humble midshipman.

As a "snotty", he was treated with little or no respect and was frequently kicked, cuffed and given a severe rollicking. His naval career lasted 20 years during which time he travelled the world and survived some dangerous situations. He was once off China in an open boat which came under heavy fire when attempting a landing. The boat was struck many times, the oars shot away and two ratings severely wounded. A lieutenant was hit and thrown overboard: Victor dived into the sea, dragged him back into the boat and dressed his gaping wound. Eventually, the boat was completely destroyed by gunfire. But Victor held on to the officer and both were rescued. Victor was nominated for a Victoria Cross but no award was ever made. The author Victor Hugo got to hear about the brave Victor and mentioned him in his classic book The Toilers and the Sea.

When Victor married, his wife was not allowed to take the title "princess" so he reverted to calling himself simply Count von Gleichen. His naval career was ended through ill health and he retired with the rank of captain and received a pension of half-pay. He was given the job of Governor of Windsor Castle and looked set for a gentlemanly easy life. But it was not to be. The bank which held Victor's inheritance and savings went bust and he lost everything apart from his sinecure at Windsor Castle.

Being an independent man, he refused financial assistance and decided to earn a living as a sculptor. In those days it was unheard of for a man with such a background to earn a living using his hands. After three years working and studying under the sculptor William Theed, he began to build-up his own business and Queen Victoria allowed him to build a small studio in the grounds of St. James's Palace.

When Colonel Robert Loyd-Lindsay (Lord Wantage) decided to build a monument to King Alfred and present it to the town of Wantage, he remembered Victor, whom he had met during the Crimean War, and invited him to do the work. The outcome was the magnificent statue carved from the finest Sicilian marble, for which Count Gleichen was paid £2,000.

So when you gaze on this magnificent icon in the Market Place of the pretty town of Wantage, do spare a thought for the brave, honourable and skilful man who carved it.

King Alfred's Head Bar & Bistro

The King Alfred's Head is an old Coaching Inn, nestled at the west end of the market place in the bustling market town of Wantage.
They serve good Bistro style food, well kept Real Ales, a great selection of beers, fine wines, whiskies, spirits and liqueurs.
They also serve Italian style coffee and homemade cakes for a quick bite.

To book a table, please telephone 01235 765531, or email booking@kingalfredshead.com.

The Ridgeway

There is a favourite place where I escape sometimes.
This ancient green road runs towards the west
from Chilterns to Berkshire Downs to Wiltshire green
(but never in the other direction!)
Here I can find peace and joy and beauty
in solitude and quiet, never loneliness,
and lift my spirit up to higher spheres.
All I can hear are breezes through the trees,
great clumps of beech that stand aloof and dark.
A skylark rises over cornfields, song aloft,
hovering above nest so well concealed,
that I must tread more carefully than usual.
Here and there a glimpse of deer or hare
show perfect harmony of form and colour.
Only a distant fleeting train that snakes
through chequered fields below, and returns ones mind
to reality of on-going living and the daily grind.
To the far west, the glorious comforting Cotswolds;
to north, blue misty views of Oxford's Shotover.
Sometimes I meet an earnest, backpacked man
with muddy, well-worn boots and sturdy stick.
Exchange of nods and cheery morning smiles
sufficient – humans are irrelevant up here!
The early drovers with their woolly flocks
were first to use this ancient English road,
now rutted, full of rain in winter, mud in spring,
and fringed with narrow strips of splashed, worn grass,
while further back, long copses where the pheasants hide,
and wild things undisturbed get on with life.

Joan Carter

By road: from the M4 leave at junction 15 and take the A346/A419 exit to A420. At Plough Hill roundabout, take the first exit onto the A419 heading towards Swindon/Oxford/A420. At White Hart roundabout take the third exit onto the A420. Keep left when you get to the fork At the roundabout take the first exit then turn right onto the Hollow Road. (SN7 7 for sat nav)

Great Coxwell Barn

William Morris loved Great Coxwell, but I find his famous quote "unapproachable in its dignity" only begins to describe the spirit of this place. How to name the feeling that causes an intake of breath when you first see it? I still hold the memory of that first suspended moment. I can hear the slamming of the door of my first company car. I was 22, and impressions were sharp and strong.

Great Coxwell feels monastic, with a spirituality and presence you expect from a fine cathedral. The truth is that it was built with a hard-headed economic purpose in mind, to house the harvested wealth of Beaulieu Abbey. The site also included a windmill and other buildings, which all formed part of the productive 13th century Grange, or farm. The fish ponds can still be seen behind the Barn.

The Cotswold stone outer structure is supported by solid beams, with all the carpentry work visible. Even the architecturally uninformed can work out which bits hold up which other bits.

I recommend going to see it alone, or with someone quiet, on a fine summer day late in the afternoon, when the swifts will be flashing around the eaves as the only disturbance to an all-pervading peacefulness. I went back there many years later with a lover who chatted amiably in the dim shadows under the mighty roof. I knew from that moment that we were not going to stay together.

Erica Braun

Wayland's Smithy

Wayland was the blacksmith to the Saxon gods. As well as "swords none could resist, and winged armour which carried one over the land like an eagle", he forged shoes for the gods' mightiest war horses – and for lesser mortals too, if they had the coin to pay.

Legend has it that if a horse was tethered at a certain country crossroads overnight and a penny was left on a stone nearby, next morning it would be found with a set of new shoes which never wore out.

Trudy Godfrey

From Swindon take the number 47 (Thamesdown buses) or number X47 (RH transport).

From Wantage, follow the B4507 and turn left when prompted by a brown sign for White Horse Hill and Waylands Smithy.

From Swindon, go onto the A420 heading towards Oxford, then turn right onto Townsend Road, take the first right, then turn left when you get to Ave Road. Turn right onto the B4000, then follow signs for Waylands Smithy. (SN6 8 for sat nav)

32

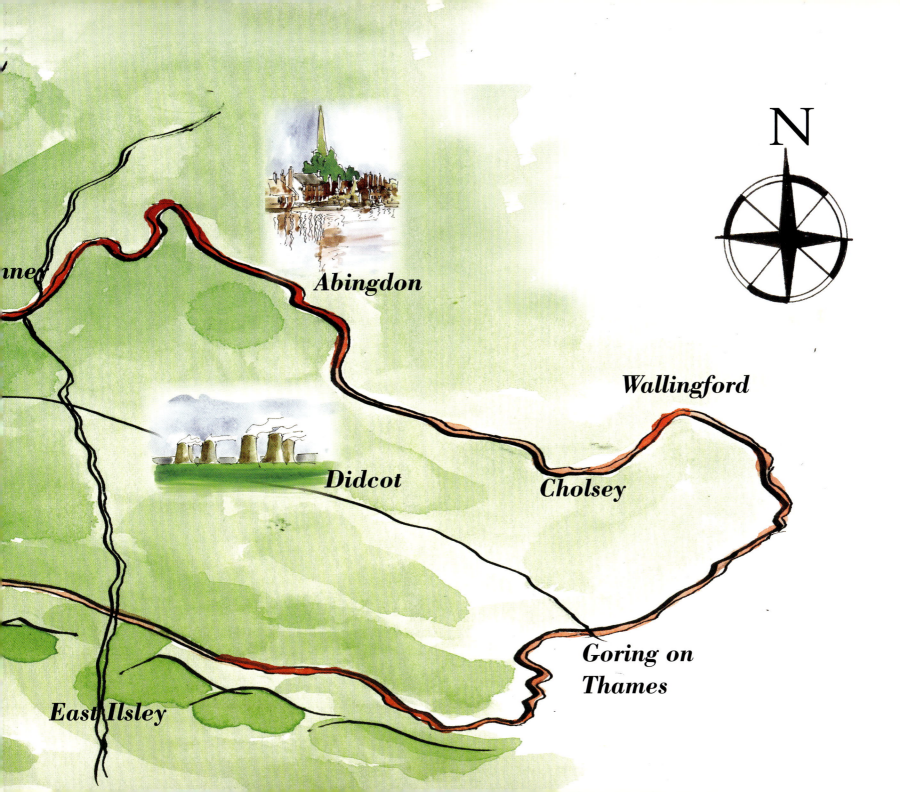

The vale of The White Horse offers some fantastic cycling opportunities down quiet country roads, in the very middle of England. The route shown here meanders through various interesting and beautiful places, past pubs and close to the cycle shops in the area – just in case!

Details of cycle rides can be viewed on www.FocusOnuk.co.uk/cycleroutes/VOWH

Local traditions; strange customs

Bun-Throwing Ceremony
Abingdon Town Council only vote to hold a Bun-Throwing to mark important royal occasions so they are rare events, accompanied by much excitement in the town. From the top of the County Hall Museum, councillors lob around 4000 currant buns, specially baked for the occasion with a crown insignia on the top. Crowds of townsfolk gather in the Market Place to catch the buns as they seemingly fall out of the sky.

Election of the Mock Mayor of Ock Street
The timing of this annual piece of Morris Dancing mayhem, on the closest Saturday to Midsummer, is a clue to its ancient roots. For many years, this was the chance for the common folk to have their (somewhat rowdy) input into the governance of the town. Ock Street was once the poorest quarter of the town and to this day the residents vote for a "mock mayor" who is carried on a litter, bedecked with flowers, from pub to pub! The dancers proudly display their symbolic cast iron cow's head and horns. It is a reminder to the lads from the other side of town that they won the fight, some 300 years ago, for the remains of the celebratory cow roast held in the Market Place.

Longest Street Fair in Europe
Abingdon's longest surviving street fair is the Michaelmas Fair. Nowadays it fills the Market Place and High Street in October, immediately followed by the Runaway Fair. The name recalls the origin of these as hiring fairs for local farmers to find new labourers and farm hands for the year. A farm hand who had found his new master cruel or the pay too low could abscond and try again at the Runaway Fair a week later.

Market Towns
The market towns in the Vale of the White Horse are all charming, picturesque places which are steeped in an astonishing amount of history. Market towns such as Abingdon, Faringdon and Wantage have their own unique identity and characteristics and prove to be very popular. The markets take place every week and date back to the 14th Century.

Swan Upping
Swan Upping is a census of the swan population along the Thames, starting from Sunbury in Surrey and completed in Abingdon, Oxfordshire. The annual ceremony of Swan Upping dates from the twelfth century when the Crown claimed ownership of all mute swans. It is the Sovereign's Swan Marker's duty to count the number of young cygnets each year. He will assess signs of injury or disease and ensure that the swan population is maintained and protected.

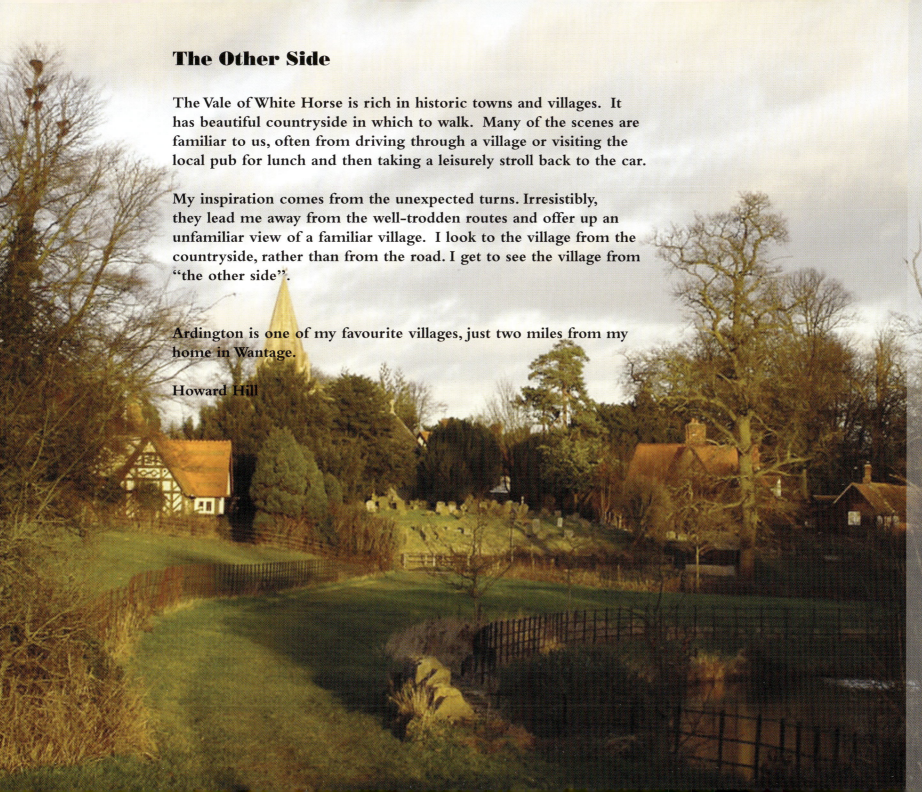

The Other Side

The Vale of White Horse is rich in historic towns and villages. It has beautiful countryside in which to walk. Many of the scenes are familiar to us, often from driving through a village or visiting the local pub for lunch and then taking a leisurely stroll back to the car.

My inspiration comes from the unexpected turns. Irresistibly, they lead me away from the well-trodden routes and offer up an unfamiliar view of a familiar village. I look to the village from the countryside, rather than from the road. I get to see the village from "the other side".

Ardington is one of my favourite villages, just two miles from my home in Wantage.

Howard Hill

From Oxford
Leave A34 at Milton Interchange, branch left then at roundabout take 4th exit onto A4130 signposted Wantage. At next roundabout take 3rd exit onto A417. Continue forward and take left turn signposted Lockinge and Ardington.

From Faringdon
Leave A420 at Stanford Road roundabout and take 2nd exit onto A417 towards Wantage. Turn right onto Vicarage Hill signposted Letcombe Regis. Turn left onto Ickleton Road B4507. At traffic signals turn left and immediately right onto A338 signposted Newbury. At first mini-roundabout branch right, then at second one continue forward onto A417 signposted Didcot A4130. At mini-roundabout continue forward then next one take second exit onto A417 signposted Oxford. Turn right signposted Lockinge and Ardington.

Earth Trust

Connect with nature, stroll through woodlands, walk around lakes and learn about sustainable living …
The Earth Trust was set up in 1969 by the British engineer Sir Martin Wood to promote environmental conservation through land management, education and land science.

It is a charity based at Little Wittenham, just outside Abingdon and manages a 1200 acre estate, which includes the Wittenham Clumps, Little Wittenham Nature Reserve, a conservation farm and an area of woodland dedicated to forestry research. There are great sites to visit; exciting things to see and a whole range of activities that one can get involved in, allowing us to reconnect to the natural world. The Earth Trust is about people and the way they feel, think and act towards the environment, encouraging them to make a difference by showing how we can live sustainably and encourage everyone to put this into practice through their daily lives, thus creating a better future.

You can discover new skills with opportunities to volunteer both practically on site, carrying out habitat management tasks, and in our offices helping with fundraising. Earth Trust also offers a number of courses and activities that you can get involved in including Bushcraft, Wilderness Cookery, Woodcraft and traditional countryside skills like hedge laying, plant identification or Coppicing. Whichever activity you choose, it is a chance to get outdoors in stunning landscape, meet lots of people and have a great time.

The Trust has many stunning views to see and unusual places for you to explore. You can get close to spectacular wildlife and watch the Trust's progress as wildflower meadows and wetland landscapes are restored. As red kites and buzzards compete for the skies above, take a walk up the hills through the wildflower meadow surrounding the Wittenham Clumps. Notice the curved ramparts and ditches of Castle Hill dating from the Iron Age and archaeological work has shown that Castle Hill was also the site of an earlier Bronze Age hill fort.
"The Clumps", have inspired poets and artists alike. Local poet Joseph Tubb carved a wonderful poem in the bark of a beech tree on Castle Hill in the years 1844-45. Today it's only possible to decipher a handful of letters but a nearby plaque allows visitors to feel the passion that this Victorian vandal had for the local landscape and its history. Another who was inspired by the Clumps was the landscape artist Paul Nash who painted the clumps many times during his career.

You can allow yourself to really connect with the Oxfordshire countryside through the meandering path of the Broad Arboretum which takes you through a living library which has every tree and shrub species native to Oxfordshire and many early introductions as well, 49 species in total.

You may stumble across, to your surprise, a 14 metre long model of a battleship, if you happen to be wandering through Neptune Wood. It is in fact a model of the 19th century battleship HMS Neptune woven using 1400 willow rods and the efforts of over 200 school children. This and the woodland of 10,000 French, Spanish and British oak trees were created to honour the 200th anniversary of the Battle of Trafalgar; commemorating the tens of thousands of trees used to construct naval vessels.

To find complete serenity, Thrupp Lake, nestling on the outskirts of Abingdon is a beautiful haven for wildlife and is highly valued by local residents and naturalists. Thrupp Lake is magical at any time of year: In spring the trees begin to blossom, herons gather, cygnets hatch and kingfishers dart by. During summer the lake shimmers with emergent damselflies and darting dragonflies. In autumn the trees give spectacular colour with swan gliding beneath them, and a winter's mist or snow can transform the lake into a magical wetland attracting a multitude of birds nesting over winter.

The circular walk around the lake allows for a gentle stroll and many interesting places to see: A wooden boardwalk giving you the opportunity to walk over water; A bird hide that blends in to the surroundings allowing you to watch and photograph any skittish birds without disturbing them, and a wonderful wooden shelter shaped like a water lily in bloom providing warm and dry seating on windy days so that you can enjoy your view of the lake without any disturbance.

The Earth Trust estate is a fabulous place to take the family. The handsome setting of the countryside, lakes and wildlife sums up the beautiful natural world we tend to forget and we should help look after.

www.earthtrust.org.uk

From Abingdon, depart on the B4017 / Bath Street toward Yewtree Mews, turn left onto A415 / Stratton Way then keep right to stay on A415 / Stert Street. Turn right onto High Street then turn left onto local roads for 1 mile and then take the right hand turn onto Little Wittenham Road.

Little Wittenham,
Abingdon,
Oxfordshire,
OX14 4QZ
01865 407792

From M4 exit at junction 15 towards Plough Hill roundabout. Take the third exit onto the A419 heading towards Swindon. At the roundabout take the second exit onto Merlin Way heading towards Swindon. At the White Hart roundabout take the third exit onto the A420 heading towards Oxford. Keep left at the fork then turn right onto The Hollow Road. Take the First exit onto the B4019 then turn right and Badbury Clumps will be on your right.

Badbury Clumps

Badbury Clumps is a wonderful natural beauty spot just outside Faringdon. There is a mix of tall deciduous trees above a carpet of bluebells in the Spring. However, walk deeper into the forest – to the older part – that is home to ancient Scots pines. No matter how many times you do this walk, and whatever the season, your senses tell you that you have crossed into the older part of the forest. It becomes darker, more foreboding and feels a little dangerous. This is when the true age of the forest (home to an Iron Age fort) becomes clear. Listen carefully and you can hear the forest tell you its secrets. We like to combine a trip to Badbury Clumps with a well deserved coffee with home made cake in one of the Faringdon coffee-shops!

Trudy Godfrey

A Church there is

St. Augustine's church, located in the pretty village of East Hendred, is a lovely church with a pleasant atmosphere. The entry for Hennrithe (East Hendred) in the Domesday Book, 1087, simply states 'a church there is'. No evidence of the original structure survives. The origins of the present church are around 1200 AD or just before then. The Early English arcade with the wonderful foliated capitals indicates this fact.

The John Seymour faceless clock may be seen in the tower. Dated 1525, it is still going strong and receiving visitors from all over the world. Standing in the Eyston Chapel is a Reformation wooden altar. The Eyston Chapel, built around 1450 AD, includes a wealth of fine monuments and the original massive oak screen survives. The chapel began as a chantry and remained the burial chapel for the Eyston family until the 19th Century.

In 1649, King Charles I was executed. After eleven years of military dictatorship under Oliver Cromwell, amid great rejoicing, the monarchy was restored in 1660 AD, when Charles II returned from exile. The marvellously carved East Hendred Restoration pulpit, is our memorial to Charles I whose carved Van Dyck-style effigy can be seen. The pulpit is richly carved and possesses an equally richly carved canopy. Interestingly, an ugly effigy of Oliver Cromwell may be seen on the panel facing the north transept.

The unusual lectern, still in use after more than eight hundred years, is sometimes called a Crusader Lectern but the duration of the Crusades does not help us date it. The lectern has two reading postures, kneeling and standing and is in the shape of a mailed leg and foot. The foot may be seen stamping on three dragons' heads. This is believed to represent the triumph of good over evil. On either side towards the top you can see an oak leaf representing strength and a willow branch which may indicate a crusader's staff.

Norman Francis

From Oxford head southbound on the A34 and take the A4130 towards Chilton/A417. At the Milton interchange take the fourth exit onto the A4130 heading towards Wantage. At the roundabout take the third exit onto the A417 then turn left onto Orchard Lane. Take the first exit onto Chapel Square. The church will be on your right.

From the south leave the M4 at junction 13, take the A34 exit to Oxford/Newbury. At the roundabout take the third exit onto the A34 ramp to Oxford/Chieveley. Exit the A34 onto the A4185 towards Wantage. At the roundabout take the first exit onto the A417. Turn left onto White Road. Take the third right onto Orchard Lane then take first left onto Chapel Square. (OX12 8NJ for satnav)

To market to market

Sometimes it feels as though markets were invented in this part of the world. Our market towns are built for them, with delightful central squares and market halls. More importantly, our communities love them, enabling around thirty established markets in Southern Oxfordshire to thrive.

With the roof canvasses flapping in the breeze, fresh produce stacked up on the tables and the traders in full swing, there is nothing quite like a local market for putting the zing back into shopping and re-connecting you with local food and local entrepreneurs.

Markets are becoming the preferred outlet of many a talented young designer. Angela Palterman sells her stunning jewellery through her own company, Posh Pebbles. Using a modern combination of internet marketing and a regular presence at markets like the Wallingford Friday market, she delights customers with a range of beautiful stones in simple but elegant designs, at affordable prices.
www.facebook.com/PoshPebbles
poshpebbles@live.com
07788824527

Mark and Debbie Warder are the craftspeople behind Designs in Glass, to be seen at Abingdon's Local Excellence Market, and monthly at Wallingford's Local Producers Market. On a market day, they display and sell decorative and functional tableware pieces in kiln-formed glass which sparkle in the sunshine. In addition Debbie and Mark also design, create, repair and restore all manner of stained glass and lead lights, working for both domestic and commercial customers, undertaking commissions large and small. They give free quotes and advice, working closely with clients, allowing plenty of input at all stages of the creative process. The markets provide an opportunity to meet them informally to discuss any aspect of their work.
www.designs-in-glass.co.uk
Tel 01865 739675

Abingdon Market which is held every Monday, with a Farmers' Market every third Friday of the month.

Wantage Market has two weekly markets held, with one every Wednesday and one every Saturday.

Wantage Farmers' Market is held on the last Saturday of the month.

Faringdon Market takes place every Tuesday with a Farmers' Market on the first Tuesday of the month.
Fernham has a Farmers' Market which takes place at Farmer Gow's near Faringdon. They are on the 3rd Sunday of every month.

Vale and Downland Museum - Wantage

The attractive Grade II listed building, home of the Vale and Downland museum, is rather like Doctor Who's 'Tardis'; small on the outside, but seemingly endless and packed with exciting discoveries on the inside. Many of these discoveries are designed with 'little hands' in mind and children are encouraged to push buttons on an interactive 3D map of the Vale, make fossil tracings, play with electronic trains and dress up as King Alfred.

The museum galleries tell the 'story' of the Vale of White Horse: from fossils to Formula One. Sit back and let David Attenborough introduce you to the area and discover how the Vale's geology has shaped the growth of surrounding towns and villages. Wander through the family friendly exhibits to discover the trades that made Wantage a thriving town. Experience the first steam passenger tram in Britain, find out how to cook in a Victorian kitchen, dress up like an Anglo-Saxon and appreciate the sophisticated technology of a Formula One car.

This intriguing and child friendly museum provides an ideal way to spend four hours finding out about the history of the Vale, with its ancient monuments and artifacts, strange customs and traditions. The cosy café provides delicious lunches and home-made cakes that prove very successful in tempting visitors to stay a little bit longer!

Williams Formula 1 is of special importance because the Williams F1 Conference Centre is located just outside of Wantage, and provides a suitable destination for some of the finest Grand Prix cars ever built once they've served their term in the sport.

Messing about on the Letcombe Brook

Memories of an idyllic childhood conjure up images of messing about in sun-dappled streams, catching sticklebacks with friends or spotting the vibrant blue streak of a kingfisher as it flashes past. Whether or not you actually experienced these opportunities as a child, it's never too late to start and Letcombe Brook is a great place to begin.

The Brook is a chalk stream that flows through the Vale of the White Horse. Chalk streams are globally rare but sixty four per cent of them flow through the UK countryside. Their crystal clear waters are rich in biodiversity and Letcombe Brook plays host to wild brown trout, bullhead fish and freshwater shrimps. England's most endangered mammal, the water vole, also calls Letcombe Brook home as do otters, one of our most endearing animals. Their return is due to the work carried out by the Letcombe Brook Project and its partners that have helped improve the habitats and water quality.

There are plenty of places to enjoy the Letcombe Brook. It flows twelve kilometres through villages, town and farmland and is a prominent feature. Rising at the spring line villages of Letcombe Regis and Letcombe Bassett you can visit the Letcombe Valley Nature Reserve, or a take a walk by the brook at Mill Street in the market town of Wantage and at the village green in Grove. A footpath will take you north following the brook through East Hanney.

If history is more your thing, take a stroll along the Brook where you can still see some of the mills that used its water to provide power. The Brook still provides water for domestic, industrial and agricultural use today. Clarkes Mill in Wantage was used to grind corn, and silk was spun at Dandridge's Mill in East Hanney. People long ago chose to settle along the Brook as it provided a clean and plentiful supply of fresh water and power.

Sally Wallington

Heading south from the A34, take the exit at the Botley Interchange. At the Interchange take the third exit onto the A420. At Tubney roundabout take the first exit onto the A338. Go through 3 roundabouts. Turn right onto Wallingford Street/A417. Then take the third exit onto Market Place/A417. Then turn left onto market place/A338. Take the first right onto Church Street. If coming from the M4, exit at junction 14. At the roundabout take the exit toward onto Baydon Road/A338 heading towards Wantage. Continue to follow the A338. Turn left onto Newbury road/A338. Take the first right onto Wantage road/A338. Continue to follow the A338 until you are in Wantage. Turn left onto Church Street. (OX12 8 for satnav)

44

Faringdon

Faringdon is a quirky little town. It is sometimes also known as "Great Faringdon" or "Chipping Faringdon" because of its market and to distinguish it from Little Faringdon. It is a fantastic place full of history and character.

Faringdon, a name derived from "fern-covered hill", is mentioned in the Domesday Book and has a long and varied history with evidence of habitation by prehistoric Man, Romans, Saxons, Normans and Vikings. King Alfred had a Saxon Palace near All Saints Church and apparently famously burnt his cakes here.

In 1202, King John donated the Royal Manor of Faringdon with permission to build an Abbey, and later transferred ownership to the famous Abbey at Beaulieu in the New Forest. Most of the monks transferred to Beaulieu although some stayed to build the Tithe Barn at Great Coxwell. Legend has it that King John's gift of land for a monastery came after a time when he was whipped for having shown a lack of respect to the Cistercian Monks.

In 1218, King Henry III gave the town a Royal Charter to hold a weekly market which is still held every Tuesday.

A number of famous battles took place in the town with particularly prominence in the English Civil War. Faringdon was one of the last places in England to hold out for the King and, although Cromwell briefly occupied the town in 1645 attacking the royalist battalion defending All Saints Church and Faringdon House, he was unsuccessful in taking control. By the end of the Civil war the town was all but destroyed. Parliament declared it, and Torrington in Devon, the two worst war-damaged towns in England. The spire at All Saints had been blown to pieces and there still remains a cannon ball embedded in the east wall.

Faringdon House was for many generations home to the Pye family. Their most renowned member was the 18th Century poet laureate Sir Henry James Pye, referred to in the nursery rhyme "Sing a Song of Sixpence. Another of the family is said to haunt the churchyard at All Saints. The headless ghost of Sir Robert James Pye's son, John Hampden, is said to wander locally to haunt his step mother who ordered his head "blown off" at sea.

The number of pubs for one town (up to 36) is also a striking piece of history. The Old Coaching Inn dates back to the 12th Century and has a tunnel which leads from the cellar to All Saints Church. The Red Lion is famous for being mentioned in Tom Browns Schooldays. A historic piece of prose written by Rosa May, for her son, in 1896 describes them:

"Driving through the town of Faringdon one day, I was delighted to find a very old and valued friend, the DUKE OF WELLINGTON and, having shaken hands with him by way of salutation, we proceeded down Gloster (sic) Street escorted by THE VOLUNTEER, made the best of our way to the MARLBOROUGH ARMS, having seated ourselves for a drink, the landlord informed us that the angel had seen the crown knocked out of the queens arms by the DUKE OF YORK.

Determined to see if such a thing were true we started away to Coxwell Street and there we met the GARDENER with the WHEATSHEAF in his arms, just preparing to feed The Swan. We asked him if such a thing were true, he did not think so but he informed us that THE RED LION has been chasing THE EAGLE and THE EAGLE was now at the top of the street and THE RED LION was now chasing THE WHITE HART all round The Folly.

Away we started again and when we got to the market place we were alarmed to hear the tolling of THE BELL and enquiring what was the matter we were told that THE OLD BULL had been and kicked THE STAR over in to THE BAKER'S ARMS.

Finis"

Of the above, only The Angel, The Bell, The Old Crown, The Duke of Wellington, The Red Lion, The Swan, The Volunteer, The Wheatsheaf and The Folly are still open today.

The town is probably best known for being the home of the eccentric. The Pink Pigeon Trust was born to bring out the creative side of the town, in the spirit of Lord Berners, and seeks to be influence activities throughout the year including the Arts Festival. You might not get to have tea with a giraffe in one of our great local cafés but you will see some pink pigeons.

Daniel Pullen Walenn

From Oxford
Take A420 towards Faringdon. About 2 miles after Littleworth, take a right signed Faringdon Market Square.

From Swindon
Take A420 towards Faringdon. About 1.5 miles from Faringdon pass the Great Coxwell and Faringdon Town Centre turns. Continue along by pass taking a left turn signed to Faringdon Market Square.

Be still. Watch. Listen.
Draw your coat about you, wait.
The shadows move toward us,
The stillness descends upon us.
The pale moon edges though the clouds.
From afar, the unmistakable wing-beat,
pulsating.
She settles.
The quiet resumes.
The clouds fold over the fading moon.
Dark.

Challow & Childrey

Many leave Wantage, eager to see Uffington, its quaint Museum, the famous White Horse and other historic sites along the Ridgeway. In their haste, they may well pass by one of the best "view points" in the county.

On leaving Wantage on the B4507, up the hill past East Challow, take care to look over your shoulder to see the view over Wantage to Didcot. As you top the rise, the hedges on the left give way to reveal the beautiful view of the Ridgeway over the Letcombe villages. Don't look for too long save you miss the sudden opening of the amazing view to the right. At the top of West Challow hill, take in the sweep of the Ridgeway down into the vale, with Childrey and West Challow close by. The panoramic view stretching for miles from Faringdon on the left, following the distant horizon all the way across to the Oxford hills to the right, makes an intriguing patchwork of fields, hedges and roads.

This forever changing view reflects the seasons, the weather and the farming. Even after 32 years I still stop on my way home for a little magical inspiration.

Joyce Bunting,

Wantage to Letcombe walk

One of my favourite walks is the path from Wantage to Letcombe Regis.

It starts off as a single track road and ends in a simple pathway edging open fields. The ever changing light and colours have been a source of inspiration to me and I have made numerous paintings and sketches of this unique environment.

As winter turns to spring you are greeted with delicate greens filtering the blue light coming off the downs. In high summer it is a mass of colours with purple shadows and pink highlights.

Stuart Roper

www.widcombehouse.co.uk

From the market place you exit on the Hungerford road. Straight across the traffic lights on Newbury street.

Willow lane can be found on the right hand side opposite the entrance to Manor Road Park.

The path goes past the back of the leisure centre, past a small group of allotments, where it narrows to a track in an avenue of trees. Follow the path over a small bridge where it bends to the right and skirts the edge of a field.

The path finishes on the outskirts of the Village of Letcombe regis.

Total distance approximately 1 mile. The path is accessible for pushchairs and cycles. Though some parts can get a little muddy in winter.

Island Hopping in the Vale

The villages of West and East Hanney do not have the obvious attractions of the spring-line villages of the Letcombes or the Hendreds, but they do have their own charms. Those who make the effort to explore their lanes and footpaths will be well rewarded.

The Hanneys, along with Goosey, Charney and Pusey are known as "the island villages", the 'ey' ending to the village name being a clue, meaning island. In former times, the Hanneys would have been damp, isolated communities. The terrain; marshy and boggy and the heavy clay soil a discouragement to casual visitors walking or riding down the tracks from Grove and Wantage, or across the causeway from Steventon and Abingdon.

Nowadays East Hanney is by-passed by the busy Wantage/Oxford Road (A338), and West Hanney is connected by narrow roads to the Wantage/Faringdon Road (A417), so access to both villages is straightforward. Parking is available in the village hall car park.

You can follow the raised pavement, The Causeway, to West Hanney Village Green where you will see the renovated Butter Cross, of mediaeval origins. It was either a market cross or maybe a marked boundary. There was a time when this cross had almost disappeared and most of the stones had ended up in villagers' gardens and walls. In 1908, Mr Large of Pound Croft, East Hanney, undertook the mammoth task of re-locating most of the stones and re-assembling the cross. His work stands for us to admire today.

From the Green, bear left and walk along the raised and flagged path, (which proved its worth in the 2007 floods!), leads past West Hanney House. The origin of this house is unknown, but it may have been part of a monastic estate. The present house was built in the 1720s and was owned by the diocese of Salisbury until 1887. See the replica windows, painted to avoid the old Window Tax. The most prominent building in the village is the huge church of St James the Great, built on Saxon foundations. If you enjoy visiting churches this one is well worth a visit. You will enter the building through the perfect Norman doorway behind which you will see the Norman font decorated with over a hundred flowers carved in vertical mouldings. On the floor of the chancel is one of the best collections of brasses in the county, if not the country, dating from 1370.

Close to the church is the 17th Century oak-beamed pub, The Plough and the fine building of Priors Court which stands beside the church. This stone-built house is of Jacobean date but originally was the site of a Benedictine settlement established by Walter de Gifard in early Norman times.

On the far side of the village you will come to Wests Mill, also known as Lower Mill. The water wheel has been removed and the building is now a private house. During the Napoleonic Wars, French prisoners of war carried on a silk weaving business here. The mill returned to its traditional uses at the end of the war. To the left is one of the most interesting houses in the village, Philberds Manor. One of the biggest and most rambling houses in the county, it was burnt down as recently as 2007. It has now been magnificently rebuilt and restored to its former glory. This manor, in name only, dates back 700 years. At one time it was the home of the detested Sir William Scroggs who became Lord Chief Justice in 1678.

A short walk away you will see some interesting old houses, as well as several modern ones, many with charming gardens: East Hanney Green with its beautiful terrace of what were, formerly, five thatched cottages (some say more). Take a narrow footpath between two houses. This will bring you to what was, until recent times, a Chapel-at-Ease known as St James the Less. This building was built in 1856 by the famous Victorian architect GE Street for the parishioners of East Hanney. In 1977 the chapel was declared redundant and is now a private house.

A short walk down the Medway is The Black Horse pub and, a little further on, a fine house on the right called The Mulberries. From around 1891 until his death, in 1938, this house was occupied by James Holmes and his family. A full account of his life can be read in "Holmes of Hanney" by Frank Poller. Born and bred in the Hanneys, it is of interest to note that he was much preoccupied with population issues and was a pioneer supplier of birth control aides. During the Boer War James Holmes became very unpopular in the village due to his pro-Boer views. There were many village families with sons fighting in South Africa. In April 1900 a crowd of several hundred besieged the house, breaking all of the windows and burning an effigy of Mr Holmes. It must have been a frightening experience for the family.

Further on you come to Dandriges Mill, which stands on the bridge spanning the Letcombe Brook. The building was recently adapted into several apartments but, in its heyday, when flour was ground to be delivered to Oxford bakeries, up to thirty people worked there. During the second world war the premises were used to make aircraft equipment.

Not far from the village shop, and the allotments, is and old iron bridge from where you can enjoy an outstanding view of Letcombe Brook: tranquil and serene.

Angela Cousins
Resident in West Hanney for forty years

Head west out of Oxford along A420. At Tubney Wood Roundabout take the first exit onto the A338 signposted Wantage. Turn right onto Summertown. Turn left onto Mill Orchard. Bear right onto Brookside. Turn left onto The Causeway.

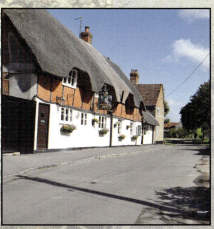

Uffington

The village of Uffington lies on the edge of the Vale of the White Horse, just north of the Berkshire Downs. Overlooking the village is the famous White Horse, a marvellous chalk figure cut into the hillside 3000 years ago.

The village has a fine church, known as The Cathedral of the Vale, and an excellent museum.

Uffington has literary connections too. John Betjeman, Poet Laureate, lived in the village and Thomas Hughes, author of Tom Brown's School Days, was born at Uffington vicarage. Several of Hughes' books are based on local people and places; the museum is actually housed in the school featured in his most famous work.

Peggy and Roger Martin

The 67 links Uffington with Faringdon, Wantage and Stanford-in-the-Vale. Saturday bus run by Thamesdown Transport between Swindon and Uffington.

From the north via the A34, take the exit towards Botley Interchange. At Botley Interchange take the third exit onto the A420. At Tubney Wood roundabout take the first exit onto the A338. Turn left onto Main Street and take the first right towards Goosey lane. Turn right onto A417 and take the first left onto Baulking Lane and then straight onto Station road. Turn right onto White Horse and Uffington Village.

From the M4, exit at junction 14 and at the roundabout, take the third exit onto Baydon Road/A338 heading towards Wantage. Turn left onto Baydon Road/B4000. Continue to follow the B4000 and turn right to stay on the B4000. Take the B4001 and turn left towards Blowingstone Hill and then turn left towards Fawler road. Continue straight onto Fawler road and the White Horse and Uffington Village.
(SN7 7RP for satnav)

Buscot Park for an out-of-this-world experience in a by-gone grandiose era

Extraordinary art and beautifully landscaped gardens sit side by side at Buscot Park, one of those very special places in the west of the Vale that is always worth a visit. The National Trust estate at Buscot is not only home to the Faringdon Collection, a rich varied and evergrowing collection of art, artefacts and sculptures, but also to some of the finest landscaped gardens in the country with many distinguishing features including the Italianate Peto Water Garden, built in the early years of the 20th century, which links the house to the Big Lake through waterways with paths, basins and stairways and the more recent Four Seasons Walled Garden with its four quadrants with a statue by Frank Forster in each corner and a central lily pond.

There is always something new to catch the eye at Buscot, recently a small army of Chinese terracotta warriors appeared, replicas of five different ranks of the Great Army discovered at Xi'an, hidden from view until the visitor suddenly comes upon them on the Stairway. Elsewhere visitors come across the circular Swinging Garden, a great place to sit, swing, relax and gather thoughts. There is the Faux Fall water feature that catches the eye from a distance as well as many fine vistas across the parkland, but visitors need to allow enough time to cover the extensive grounds and the house itself and fortunately there is an excellent tea room which is open when both house and gardens are.

Entering the house, which was first built in the 1780s, is like entering a different world. Visitors enter the Hall to be greeted by waxed stone flags and two beautiful pillars and the Egyptian influenced couch and pair of chairs.

Turning to the Dutch Room there is one of the collection's best known works, Rembrandt's portrait of Pieter Six. Perhaps the jewel in the collection is The Saloon, a room that has no match anywhere, which contains Burne-Jones's illustration of the story of the Sleeping Beauty 'The Legend of the Briar Rose', a series of four paintings which dominates the neo-classical room.

There is so much to see and take in inside Buscot House that one visit may not be enough to give full justice to the house and the parklands and there is not much point hurrying as important things will be missed. Some of its treasures can be glimpsed on the website, but there is no substitute for a personal visit. This is an enchanted and peaceful oasis, under the guiding hands of Lord and Lady Faringdon.
As one visitor put it in the comments book," Probably the most beautiful National Trust property we have ever been in." Another said "A beautiful and excellent collection of art."

The Buscot Park website gives many more details about the exquisite works of art in the Faringdon Collection, the features of the park and visitor information.
www.buscotpark.com and www.visitvale.com

Buscot Park is just 3 miles outside of the beautiful market town of Faringdon on the A417 on the way to Lechlade.

The nearest rail station is at Swindon (10 miles away), while a number of bus services operate to Lechlade: Thamesdown 67 Swindon-Faringdon (Fridays only); Carterton 64 Swindon-Carterton; Thamesdown 77 Swindon-Cirencester (both the last two services pass close to the rail station in Swindon).

The 67 and 77 services only go to Lechlade: alight here, there is then a 2 3/4 mile walk to Buscot Park.

The Radnor Arms, Coleshill

Sitting just inside Oxfordshire's border with Wiltshire is the picturesque National Trust village of Coleshill. On the main road through the village, the B4019, sits the Radnor Arms, which is home to the Old Forge Brewery, an award winning micro-brewery.

Its name comes from the Earls of Radnor who once lived at nearby Coleshill House. In World War 2 the house was used as a secret base to train the Auxiliary Units - the secret network of volunteer men and women prepared to be Britain's last ditch line of defence, but sadly burnt down in a huge infamous fire in the summer of 1952, caused by a painter's blowtorch.

Before it became a pub in 1949 it was the estate blacksmiths and there is much evidence of this in the Smithy bar, which is festooned with various metalwork artefacts. One of the brewery's regular real ales is called Old Ted, named affectionately after a former blacksmith, others are Sledgehammer, Hammer and Tong, Blacksmiths Gold and Anvil Ale.

The Old Forge Brewery was founded in 2010 and within a year received the accolade of being awarded the title of Camra's Oxfordshire Pub of the Year. It has a sister brewing operation in Lechlade at The Crown, the Halfpenny Brewery. www.radnorarmscoleshill.co.uk

Milletts Farm Centre

Millets Farm Centre, located just outside Abingdon, has been a family business since 1952. If you are looking for a fantastic day out for all the family then Millets will not disappoint. Come once, and we guarantee you will become a regular visitor.

For the children there is a play area, a farm zoo and pick-your-own-fruit as well as seasonal events throughout the year such as the Maize Maze, Easter Eggsstravaganza, Hallowe'en Howl and Santa's Grotto. For the grown-ups, wander through the ten-acre Phoebe Wood, comprising woodland and wetland walks along the banks of the River Ock, or picnic near the Trout Lakes. If you are a foodie then visit the award winning shop selling local produce and the Farmhouse and Lakeview Restaurants that cater for visitors and functions. www.milletsfarmcentre.com

Alfred's Lodge – a well-being retreat in the heart of Wantage

Built in 1901 for Miss Elizabeth White, spinster of the parish, Alfred's Lodge is a large, rambling Victorian red brick building on Ormond Road in Wantage. The house now belongs to Jane McCourt who, with her business partner Marit Selmar-Langekar runs Compare Your Body, a company dedicated to helping people lead healthier lives. A bed and breakfast with a difference, Jane and Marit offer wellbeing retreats for those looking to relax and de-stress.

With five well appointed en-suite guest rooms, an edible garden boasting vegetables, fruits and berries as well as edible flowers, guests can unwind in a comfortable, calming environment and take advantage of individual, tailor made programmes for weight management, relaxation and improved fitness. Using the revolutionary 'turn back time' machine which measures arterial stiffness – a key health indicator – Jane and Marit advise on lifestyle changes to combat the ageing process and improve your biological age, blood pressure, BMI and arterial stiffness. Therapies available include Thai yoga massage, Pilates, fitness training, physiotherapy and life coaching.

Jane explains "I have always been interested in healthy nutrition, herbs and alternatives to traditional medicine. Having experimented with detoxing, vegan, vegetarian and raw food diets and found what suits me nutritionally, I now have a much better quality of life both physically and mentally." Although vegetarian, Jane provides a traditional English breakfast as well as vegetarian and vegan options.

Wantage is known as the Gateway to the Ridgeway, popular for cycling, running, walking and endless views, so outdoor pursuits are also available and dogs are welcome too. A stay at Alfred's Lodge is guaranteed to revive and re-energise even the most jaded constitution.

For more information contact: Alfred's Lodge, 23 Ormond Road, Wantage OX12 8EG Tel: 0845 129 0009

www.compareyourbody.com

Visit Cotswold Wildlife Park, the biggest surprise in the Cotswolds

No matter how hard you look you won't find a zebra Pushmi-Pullyu at Cotswold Wildlife Park, but you will find over 260 species of animals, birds and reptiles in acres and acres of beautiful, tranquil parkland and gardens that are easy for all ages and abilities to wander around in. The park is centred around a Georgian Manor House, just two miles south of Burford, which in 2010 celebrated its 40th anniversary.

One of the park's better known animal characters is George the Giant Tortoise, who comes originally from the Seychelles in the Indian Ocean. George is known for his curmudgeonly character and is thought to be well over 60 years old. He was one of the first animals to arrive at the park over 40 years ago. He lives in the tortoise enclosure with two females and enjoys making comments on Twitter. (@CotsWildTweets#GrumpyGeorge)

Of course there are many more animals, bird and reptiles that live in relative harmony at the spacious, relaxed park. Some of my favourites include Barney, the 15 year-old anaconda, (and a prolific father), to a newly born zebra called Rodney. But of course I also love visiting the inquisitive and sociable meerkats, red pandas, giraffes and ring-tailed lemurs.

But it's not only about animals, there are the gardens and parkland and some extraordinary trees and vegetation to enjoy at any time of year. The sheltered Walled Garden, which was formerly a kitchen garden, contains some exotic plants that flourish in the micro-climate alongside the tropical birds in the walkthrough aviary, the meerkats enclosure, monkeys and the penguin playground.

The train ride gently transports passengers on a circular ride around the grounds, so you can see beautiful places to picnic and watch the lions prowl. See if you can spot the two-humped Bactrian camels walking around in their own distinctive, yet inimitable way. There's also plenty of places for visitors to stop, have a break, find something to eat or buy a souvenir.

Cotswold Wildlife Park is a surprising place to find in the Cotswolds and its impressive investment in its ever-developing facilities is clear for all to see. The park is open every day of the year apart from Christmas Day and is one of Britain's largest zoological collections. The welfare and well-being of all its animals is a priority. It is well worth more than one visit, but if you happen to see a Pushmi-Pullyu keep it to yourself.

Ashdown House

This extraordinary building with a doll's-house appearance nestles in a beautiful valley on the Berkshire Downs, surrounded by woodland. Ashdown House is associated with the "Winter Queen" Elizabeth of Bohemia, the sister of Charles I. Along with his house at Hamstead Marshall, it is said that the William, the first Earl of Craven built Ashdown for her, but she died in 1662 before construction began.

From the top of the house you get splendid views over the downs to King Alfred's Castle, and the surrounding woodland is a delight for dog walkers.

Lambourn, Newbury, Berkshire RG17 8RE

OPAL Ladies Fashion and Lingerie - Serving Wantage's Fashionistas

Tucked away in a Georgian street behind the Market Place – OPAL Ladies fashion and Lingerie has a wonderful array of ladies fashion hand-picked from international independent designers to appeal to women of all ages, shapes and sizes. The current owners Gill and Bernard Connolly are passionate about their role as custodians of a beautiful red brick Georgian building dating from 1730 that has provided Wantage with many independent shops throughout the ages: including shoes, children's shoes and gents clothing. The name - Cripp's shoes - is etched into the brickwork above the shop and is still visible today. Today, the architecture in Newbury Street is reminiscent of a by-gone era, so it is delightful to find an up-market modern independent fashion store with such a beautiful selection of tantalizingly colourful merchandise in the window.

The business – OPAL Ladies fashion and Lingerie (formerly Marjorie's and before that Mollie Couture) has been serving customers in Wantage since 1937. I asked them to divulge the secrets of their success. Why have they thrived whilst across the UK, hundreds of independent retailers go out of business every week? They put this down to the fact that they stock a lovely range of clothing sourced from fashion shows around the country – which they select themselves – and combine this with high levels of personal service. This ranges from a personal shopping service to help customers select outfits for special occasions; to a bra-fitting service and the offer to 'order it in' within a few days is always an option. There is no question of customers having to rush red-faced through the shop partially-clothed only to find that the desired item does not come in a larger size! All desired items will be delivered to the illustrious and beautifully-lit changing cubicle, with a smile.

Francis Bacon said that "knowledge is power" and in this case, the Connolly's in-depth knowledge of what their customers want (either gleaned from customer requests, customer feedback or from their locally-held 'fashion shows') combined with their alluring window displays ensures that customers keep coming back for more.

Opal Ladies Fashion & Lingerie
2 Newbury Street, Wantage, Oxfordshire OX12 8BS
01235 762164 - Email: opal-marjories .ltd@ntlworld.com

Abingdon's Gem for Classic Car Enthusiasts - MG Car Club

One of Abingdon's most famous manufacturing success stories was the MG car factory, which operated for 50 years from 1930 to 1980 from its site in Cemetery Road. Although long gone, the historical connection to the town continues at Kimber House which is adjacent to the old factory site. It is named after Cecil Kimber, father of the MG, and is the worldwide home of the MG Car Club with its 104 affiliated clubs and over 130,000 members all over the globe.

Such is the affection and enthusiasm for the classic MG marque that Abingdon remains is the world's epi-centre for MG aficionados. For here there are historical records, photographs, artefacts, a shop area and a small team of enthusiastic people involved in keeping the MG spirit alive through organising important events in the UK tourism calendar - the MG Live at Silverstone and the locally acclaimed annual Old Speckled Hen Run. The club also produces a monthly magazine and uses its website to keep members informed of MG news.

The Old Speckled Hen Run is an annual run for 100 MGs, put on by the Abingdon Works Centre, which begins and ends at Radley College on a Sunday in late May. This celebrates a connection with another former Abingdon company, the brewers Morlands, who created a fiftieth anniversary ale 'The Old Speckled Hen' in honour of the factory runabout in 1980. In 2011 the run honoured former club president Bill Wallis, who died in 2010, who used to flag off the cars every year at Radley College.

New cars were driven out of the factory onto local roads for test drives as far as Marcham and the A420. The company were involved in racing at the famous Brooklands track in Surrey, birthplace of British motorsport, Le Mans 24 hour race for sports cars and MG speed trials on the Bonneville Salt Flats in Utah.

The MG car has been through many changes in its long history, from its early connection to William Morris (Lord Nuffield) in Oxford, to the move to Abingdon in 1929. When production ceased in Abingdon in 1980 production moved to Longbridge, but the home of the club stayed in Abingdon. Following the turbulent MG Rover era the company was acquired by the Shanghai Automotive Industry Corporation (SAIC) in 2007 and the company brought the MG6 into production in 2011. This is a fine example of collaboration between British design and Chinese manufacturing.

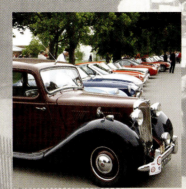

Tom Brown's School Museum,

The Museum is housed in the old schoolroom which was built in 1617 by Thomas Saunders, a wealthy merchant from Woolstone. He endowed the school with a field and two cottages to provide the necessary income for the benefit of poor and worthy boys; eight from Uffington and four from Woolstone. It remained a school until the boys were transferred in 1870 to the newly built National School. The Museum is a Grade 2 listed building.

The building features in the opening chapters of Tom Brown's Schooldays. This famous book was written by Thomas Hughes in 1857 and has never been out of print since. He grew up in the village and although he did not attend the school, he drew on his experience of village life for his books and many of the landmarks he mentioned are still in existence. As well as being an author, he was also an important social reformer of his time.

Another famous resident, Sir John Betjeman, is remembered in the Museum and we are privileged to hold copies of his correspondence in the museum for visitors to look at. Sir John Betjeman was not only a poet but a broadcaster and journalist who opened the public's eyes to the value of the buildings and landscape around them and became Britain's grand champion of its heritage.

The Museum, built of chalk ashlar with a sarsen stone base, is situated close to the church near the centre of the village. It features displays on the White Horse, other prehistoric sites and the evidence of occupation in the area for over 3000 years. Figures around the fireplace give you an idea of how the schoolroom would have appeared in Victorian times and there is a display on the 'new' school that was built in 1853.

In the Gallery there is a touch screen where you can explore the history of Uffington through an interactive display. This interactive display is also on the computer on the ground floor. In addition, there are presentations about the village and the White Horse. The exhibition in the Gallery changes each year. Whilst at the Museum you can pick up a leaflet on 'The Village Trail' which gives details of places of interest on a circular walk around the village.

The Museum is run entirely by volunteers and achieved full accreditation status by the Museums, Libraries and Archives Council in 2008. It is open from Easter to the end of October on weekends and Bank Holiday Monday afternoons from 2.00–5.00 pm.

Whilst you are visiting the Museum, you might also visit St. Mary's Church who serve teas in the Church on Sunday afternoons from June to September. Cream Teas are also served at The Teapot, Britchombe Farm near The White Horse Hill from Easter to October at weekends from 3.00 pm. There is a public house in the village: The Fox & Hounds in High Street and a pottery to visit at Shotover Corner – see The Uffington Potters www.uffingtonpotters.co.uk.

www.museum.uffington.net.
Uffington, Oxon. SN7 7RA

White Hart FYFIELD

Nestled in the village of Fyfield, tucked away in a quiet location yet, equidistant between the cities of Swindon and Oxford, the White Hart is a pub with an unusual history. It dates from 1442 and was built in the reign of Henry VI by the executors of Sir John Golafe, lord of Fyfield Manor, leaving money for the establishment of a charity to be known as the House of St John the Baptist. This early 'hostel for homeless men' provided accommodation for a priest and five almsmen (poor men) who were obliged to say masses for the soul of their benefactor to ensure his ultimate resting place in heaven. A tunnel links the current bar to the nearby manor house providing an escape route for the priest during the dissolution of monasteries.

Over the last six and a half centuries, the White Hart has been a farmhouse, sweetshop, and coaching inn. Today it is a flourishing restaurant and village pub which has recently been awarded two AA rosettes for culinary excellence. Husband and wife team, Kay and Mark Chandler believe the key to their success is their enthusiasm and passion for what they do – Mark's flair for cooking clearly helps too! Produce is locally sourced, including from the restaurant's own kitchen garden.

Their 'signature' dish is a slow roasted local pork belly served with baby spinach, carrots and apple (all from their garden of course), celeriac mash and foot-long crackling. Bedlam ensues when the pork sells out! Their hard work and consistently outstanding food has won them 'accolades a-plenty' from the Good Food Guide; the AA Restaurant Guide; the Michelin guide and Alisdair Sawday's Special Places, amongst others.

www.whitehart-fyfield.com

Diamond Light Source

For many in the Vale, the word synchrotron would have little impact. However, for the three thousand researchers from around the world who use the one based at the Harwell Science and Innovation Campus in Oxfordshire, this facility has life changing opportunities.

Diamond Light Source is one of the most advanced particle accelerator facilities in the world and can accelerate electrons to near light-speed around its 562m ring in order to generate brilliant beams of light from infra-red to x-rays. This process is then used for academic and industrial research and development in scientific disciplines ranging from physics to environmental science.

The thousands of researchers each year study all kinds of materials from artificial hips, samples of the Tudor warship, the Mary Rose, virus proteins and potential new fuel sources. This work enables scientists to:

Study protein structures to help improve cancer drugs
Investigate tissue to improve metal hip replacement technology
Develop flexible and cost efficient thin polymer films for solar cells
Develop new materials for hydrogen storage fuel cells
Study how HIV infects human cells

So, next time you pass near Harwell, spare a thought for the ground-breaking work conducted at Diamond Light Source. It could literally change your life.

Dolphin Art

Providing a friendly, informal place to browse local art and highly collectible limited editions, Dolphin Art is a gallery with an extremely high reputation in the art world.

Owners Patrick and Tara O'Leary offer a personal one-to-one service to customers, be it their first visit to the gallery or as an existing client. The couple has run the business since 1999 and recently revamped the whole shop. It is now an incredibly stylish destination shop for anyone with a fondness for art and it attracts a good number of people through its doors. Dolphin Art is unique and as well as an impressive gallery it is an art materials stockist and picture framers. It is located in the delightful and charming market place of Wantage, Oxfordshire. This thriving market town in the Vale of the White Horse was, in 849AD, the birthplace of Alfred the Great and remained a Royal Manor until the end of the 12th century. In the central market place, around which there are some fine Georgian and Victorian buildings, is a huge statue of the King.

Dolphin Art is located nearby and its reputation as a quality picture framers draws customers in from far afield. Many return for Patrick and Tara's advice and patience as they choose from the considerable collection of bespoke frames on offer. There is also a fine selection of sculptures, glassware and ceramics, which are popular with visitors.

A wide range of materials for the professional amateur artist is stocked at this wonderful gallery. For younger artists there is a fabulous range of art materials to inspire children to get stuck in and let their creativity and imaginations flow.

The Bullpen studios and gallery

The Bullpen studios and gallery is a family-run rural arts centre in Stanford in the Vale. The arts centre comprises foundry, gallery, studios and workshop room. Local artists Wesley & Helen Jacobs were among those who created the arts centre in 2005. The Bullpen has its own Foundry producing cast bronze and iron and other metalwork for and with local, national and international artists.

The galley is in a beautifully restored small, old stone barn which is connected by new-build to the studios. There are regular temporary exhibitions showing the work of leading local artists and those from further afield, exploring a range of work, techniques, disciplines and styles – all contemporary. There is also a variety workshops and classes for children, budding artists and professionals. For further information go to www.thebullpen.co.uk

When workshops are not running, visitors are welcome by appointment – just telephone ahead and the artists will happily show visitors round. There is often the opportunity to have a go, try something new or meet resident artists and see what they are making.

The Portwell Angel

In the Domesday Book of 1086, Faringdon is recorded as a manor and a mill. The town was granted a weekly market in 1218. The weekly market is still held today. King John also established an abbey in Faringdon in 1202, but it soon moved to Beaulieu in Hampshire. It seems probable that part of the Abbey buildings form the foundation of Portwell House. In the cellar, one can clearly see the old stone mullioned windows which enable one to date the building.

The picture in the background shows the Market Place in 1906 and the building on the left hand side is now the Portwell Angel.

Portwell House is "V" shaped in its construction with two pitched roofs that meet at the Market Place frontage. The valley between the two roofs is the cause of water ingress over the years. The "A" frame supporting the roof had actually rotted through when Nick Elwell & Mark Blatch acquired the building in 2009. When it was constructed, the property appears to have been built as three separate buildings now linked to provide a single premises. The top/attic floor of Portwell Cottage (one part of the building) has a fire place within it: but no means of access?

The Old Crown Coaching Inn used to be connected to Portwell House. It was separated circa 1946 when it was turned into a family home by a military man with a plethora of daughters. It subsequently became a guest house and hotel with various owners; finally closing in 1996.

During recent restoration the old fire places were opened and investigated. An intriguing internal well adjacent to one of the fire places was discovered. It is thought that the well collected rainwater from the roof – although it is not far from the well in the Crown Courtyard. The Elm floor boards were all of differing thickness – and yet were craftily laid to provide a flat (if slightly sloping!) surface. The central chimney stack and the fire place therein was closed at some point and three new chimneys created.

Much of Faringdon was destroyed by Cromwell's forces whose artillery was positioned on Folly Hill. Portwell House did not escape and was severely damaged. It appears that major works were undertaken during the 1700s (several clay pipes and a formidable looking Chaff cutter were found in the eves). Repairs and alterations since then until now have been largely superficial.

Today, the building is occupied on the ground floor by the Portwell Angel. The Portwell House Cellar is known for its cask conditioned ale. Bordengate Insurance and Focus on Faringdon CIC have taken the 1st floor and the roof space will be converted into an amazing apartment.